Especially for

....

From

....

Date

....

3-MINUTE DEVOTIONS
for Teen Girls

180 Encouraging Readings

3-MINUTE DEVOTIONS
for Teen Girls

180 Encouraging Readings

BARBOUR BOOKS
An Imprint of Barbour Publishing, Inc.

Print ISBN 978-1-63058-856-4

eBook Editions:
Adobe Digital Edition (.epub) 978-1-63409-268-5
Kindle and MobiPocket Edition (.prc) 978-1-63409-269-2

Published by Barbour Books, an imprint of Barbour Publishing, Inc., P.O. Box 719, Uhrichsville, Ohio 44683, www.barbourbooks.com

Our mission is to publish and distribute inspirational products offering exceptional value and biblical encouragement to the masses.

Member of the
Evangelical Christian
Publishers Association

Introduction

Here is a collection of thoughts from the true Source of all inspiration and encouragement—God's Word. Within these pages you'll be guided through just-right-size readings that you can experience in as few as three minutes:

Minute 1: Reflect on God's Word
Minute 2: Read real-life application and
            encouragement
Minute 3: Pray

These devotions aren't meant to be a replacement for digging deep into the scriptures or for personal, in-depth quiet time. Instead, consider them a perfect jump start to help you form a habit of spending time with God every day. Or add them to the time you're already spending with Him. Share these moments with friends, family, coworkers, and others you come in contact with every day. They're looking for inspiration and encouragement, too.

Your word is a lamp to guide my
feet and a light for my path.
PSALM 119:105 NLT

Smell Like Jesus!

He uses us to spread the knowledge of Christ everywhere, like a sweet perfume. Our lives are a Christ-like fragrance rising up to God.
2 CORINTHIANS 2:14–15 NLT

. . . .

Mmm. . .bacon! Who doesn't love the smell of bacon? The sizzling aroma permeates the entire house until every mouth waters. Even after all the bacon has been consumed, the scent clings to the house, your clothes, and your breath. You *ooze* bacon, and any outsider can immediately catch a whiff. Know what I'm talking about?

Another scent clings to you, too. The smell of Jesus! God uses His aroma to spread the knowledge of His Son to the world. Your life—your actions and words—are a sweet perfume to those around you, testifying to the goodness and love of Jesus. People catch a whiff and notice something different about you. In fact, you smell like other Christians. To some, the smell will be offensive, but to others, it will be a life-giving perfume (see 2 Corinthians 2:16).

How do you think your words and actions smell to others? Examine your heart. Are there areas of sin or stubbornness that mask your sweet *Jesus scent*? If so, clean off those foul odors and splash on a dose of Jesus perfume!

Sweet Jesus, thank You for using my life to spread the Good News to those around me. Help me to smell sweet and attractive by my words and actions today. Amen.

> *"God blesses you when people mock you and persecute you and lie about you and say all sorts of evil things against you because you are my followers. Be happy about it! Be very glad! For a great reward awaits you in heaven."*
> MATTHEW 5:11–12 NLT

. . . .

God is incredibly awesome, but not everyone believes it. When you talk about God, some people will make fun of you. When you pray to God, there is a risk of lies being spread about you. This struggle has been a part of our experience since the beginning.

Jesus makes some people uncomfortable. Many can't believe smart people follow Jesus.

These people may irritate you, and even insult you, but God says you're in good company. Pray for patience, pray for the person who irritates you, and pray for wisdom to know how to respond.

Dear God, it's not exactly the highlight of my week when someone makes fun of me. But You tell me to be glad when others reject me because of You. When this happens, I must remember they may not like my message, but they're ultimately rejecting You. Give me the strength to stand up for You and disregard the irritation. Amen.

*Get rid of all bitterness, rage, anger, harsh words,
and slander, as well as all types of evil behavior. Instead,
be kind to each other, tenderhearted, forgiving one
another, just as God through Christ has forgiven you.*
EPHESIANS 4:31–32 NLT

. . . .

It's hard to forgive people who've hurt us. While they
may need forgiveness, things like bitterness, rage, anger,
harsh words, slander, and evil behavior beg for us to
indulge the desire to hurt them in return.

Holding a grudge is like holding dynamite. At some
point someone will be hurt in the emotional explosion.
Often the one hurt (for a second time) is the grudge
holder.

We want justice for the actions of others, but grace
for our own choices. We're tough on others and easy on
ourselves. We think other people should make things
right, but we feel like we don't have to because God has
forgiven us.

*Dear God, grudges are easy to feed, grow well
on their own, and always produce a good crop.
Harsh words come easy. However, being kind and
forgiving means I give something to the offender that
they never offered. You came to give freedom through
forgiveness and love. It was Your gift. Help me give
to others what I receive from You. Amen.*

*Oh, let me warn you, sisters in Jerusalem, by the
gazelles, yes, by all the wild deer: Don't excite love,
don't stir it up, until the time is ripe—and you're ready.*
SONG OF SOLOMON 2:7 MSG

. . . .

What girl doesn't dream of love? Most of us can't wait
to feel noticed, special, and beautiful. Chances are, you'll
fall in love someday, put on a magnificent wedding gown,
and walk down the aisle to the man of your dreams. But
today is not that day. And this is not the time to stir up
the passions of your heart or body.

Song of Solomon is a beautiful poem about a man
and woman who celebrate the intimacies of love and
marriage. But three times a warning is given not to excite
such love and desires before the time is right. Yet our
culture makes it easy to be discontent and impatient for
romance.

Are you chasing after love with shallow relationships,
movies, and romance novels? Examine your heart and
determine if you need to splash cold water on your
desires by slowing down, avoiding romantic material, or
changing your perspective. Stirring up love too early only
gets you burned. Heed scripture's warning: Guard your
heart until God shows you who is worthy of receiving it.
Be content to wait for love.

*Jesus, help me guard my heart and not obsess
about boys, but to simply have fun with my
friends. Help me be content to wait. Amen.*

*God decided in advance to adopt us into his own family
by bringing us to himself through Jesus Christ. This is
what he wanted to do, and it gave him great pleasure.*
EPHESIANS 1:5 NLT

. . . .

What girl doesn't want to be a princess? I mean,
seriously. The beautiful dresses. . .the perfect hair. . .the
dashing prince. . . Yes, please! But you know what?
You *are* a princess! God the King (see 1 Timothy 6:15)
has adopted us into His family—and that makes you a
princess! He has lavishly clothed you with righteousness
(see Isaiah 61:10), made you heir of a glorious inheritance
(see Ephesians 1:18), and even provided a dashing prince
to save you while you were in distress (see Isaiah 9:6;
Romans 5:8). Wow!

The next time you feel unattractive, unworthy, or
unnoticed, remember that you are a daughter of the
King. You are greatly loved. You are special. You are
wanted. You're a *princess*.

*Almighty King, thank You for making me a real
princess! You wanted me to be part of Your family,
and my adoption gave You great pleasure. Thank You
for sending a Prince to save me from my sins.
Help me to be selfless and serving like a true princess
and share Your love with others so they can be
adopted by You, too! Amen.*

Rejoice in hope, be patient in tribulation,
be constant in prayer.
ROMANS 12:12 ESV

• • • • • • • • • • • • • • • • •

Before there were water faucets, people would go outside and use a pump to draw water from the ground. When you're thirsty, you do what needs to be done to satisfy your thirst.

Joy draws from the well of hope. Patience is produced through trial. Prayer is grown through consistency.

You'd think that joy comes from doing things that make you happy, but joy runs much deeper than happiness. Joy can be experienced on bad days, in the middle of heartbreak, and when things are at their worst. The reason this is true is that joy is energized by the hope that there will be a time when difficulties will be a thing of the past.

Patience is needed for joy to thrive because the hope that we have is all about the future. Our hope brings joy, but hope needs patience. Patience only comes by facing tough challenges.

The final connected layer is prayer. When we agree to pray regularly, we have access to the God who gave us hope, develops patience, and inspires joy. Let the rejoicing begin!

Dear God, You want me to remember that joy is something You can enhance through the struggles I face. This doesn't seem like good news. I like it when things are easy. Give me the patience to hope and the hope that inspires joy. May this prayer be a good start. Amen.

Do not be misled:
"Bad company corrupts good character."
1 CORINTHIANS 15:33 NIV

• • • • • • • • • • • • • • • • • • • •

People often use this verse to prove you need to be very careful about who you choose to be your friends. However, the bigger picture included a church where people said that Jesus didn't come back to life after He died on the cross.

If this wrong thinking had been accepted as truth then the whole idea of following Jesus wouldn't mean much. After all, if Jesus couldn't save Himself, how could He be expected to save us?

Paul was telling the people in Corinth that those who refused to believe Jesus had the ability to save were the "bad company" that "corrupts good character."

Today the idea of bad company could easily include what we watch on TV, what we read in books, and what we listen to, and it still includes people who refuse to consider that Jesus actually paid for our sins. The things we pay attention to can either help us walk with Jesus or influence us to entertain serious doubts about truth. Learn to recognize bad company.

Dear God, help me spend more time with those who love You as well as those who want to know more about You. Help me pray for those who need to know You. I don't want anything to corrupt the truth You have given in the Bible. Jesus lives, and because He lives, I have a Savior. I am grateful. Amen.

Don't get tired of helping others. You will be rewarded when the time is right, if you don't give up.
GALATIANS 6:9 CEV

. . . .

I want to love my siblings, but it's *so hard* sometimes. My brother can be such a jerk, and my sister is always taking my stuff. Why can't they just be nice or leave me alone?

And my friend that isn't saved—God, I've been praying for her *forever*. But it doesn't seem like it's made a difference. Nothing I say or do seems to prod her toward accepting You.

It all just seems so. . .hopeless, sometimes. Like no matter how hard I try to love others, it doesn't make a difference.

Well, I guess that's not entirely true. My brother does watch out for me and defend me when others pick on me. And my sister does share the TV with me so I can watch what I want to watch. Who knows? Maybe my friend will finally agree to come to youth group with me this week.

God, help me to keep serving others, even when it seems like I'm not making a difference. And help me to keep loving them, even when it's hard and I don't feel like it.

Lord, thank You for reminding me not to give up. I'm so discouraged sometimes, but I know I'll see a difference if I'm willing to keep going. Please give me strength and encouragement when I need it. Amen.

I know how to live on almost nothing or with everything.
I have learned the secret of living in every situation,
whether it is with a full stomach or empty,
with plenty or little. For I can do everything
through Christ, who gives me strength.
PHILIPPIANS 4:12–13 NLT

• • • • • • • • • • • • • • • • • •

Being satisfied with what God provides is the best way to hang on when things get tough.

Paul said he lived through times when he had everything he needed, but he also lived through challenges that left him with little. He *learned the secret of living in every situation*. That secret was satisfaction in the God who provides.

We may want to give up, throw up our hands, and admit defeat. But God didn't send us a note indicating He's no longer able to take care of things.

As long as God is in control, there's no need to panic or surrender to despair.

Because Jesus gives us strength, we can watch that strength overcome our weakness. This is where we find the encouragement to resist giving up.

Dear God, You've always been in control, and You'll be in control forever. It can be easy to think everything is falling apart. When I'm satisfied that You love me enough to take care of me, I discover that when You're with me, there is nothing that cannot be done if You want it to be done. Help me trust You more and worry less. Amen.

Don't become so well-adjusted to your culture that you fit into it without even thinking. Instead, fix your attention on God. You'll be changed from the inside out. . . . Unlike the culture around you, always dragging you down to its level of immaturity, God brings the best out of you, develops well-formed maturity in you.

ROMANS 12:2 MSG

· · · · · · · · · · · · · · · · · ·

The media puts a lot of pressure on you to dress a certain way, be a certain weight, and look gorgeous all the time. Models are airbrushed and digitally altered to portray an impossible standard of beauty. Even at school, you feel pressured to dress, speak, and act a certain way if you want to fit in and be accepted.

But God's way is different from the world. He accepts you the way you are—because He made you that way! He's far more concerned with your inner beauty, your character and attitude, than with how you appear on the outside. Spending time with Him will bring out the best in you.

As a Christian, you're supposed to be different, and that difference is Christ inside you, shining a light to others. That's a *good* thing!

God, sometimes I just want to conform, to be like the other girls, so I'll be accepted. But I really want to be who You made me to be. So help me to ignore what the world says I should do and just pay attention to what You want me to do. Amen.

*"For I was hungry and you gave me food,
I was thirsty and you gave me drink, I was a stranger
and you welcomed me."*
MATTHEW 25:35 ESV

. . . .

Jesus was an amazing storyteller. He'd been telling
His disciples about a king who spoke to two groups of
servants. Some were on his left and the others on his
right. To the first group, the king said that because they
offered help to those in need, it was like helping him. The
second group was criticized for their lack of compassion.

Jesus made it clear He wanted His disciples to be
active and involved in providing help to children, widows,
strangers, and the homeless. He referred to these willing
servants as righteous. However, He said that those who
didn't help really didn't reflect the character of His
Father.

There are many opportunities for us to help others.
We work because we want to serve God, but also
because by serving others we are letting God love them
through our actions.

*Dear God, You made it clear You want me to help.
It makes a difference when I understand that You love
every person I help. When I help them, I help You.
When I help You, I receive help. May I see others
the same way You do and care for
them like You would. Amen.*

Do not be yoked together with unbelievers...what fellowship can light have with darkness?...What does a believer have in common with an unbeliever?. . .
For we are the temple of the living God.
2 CORINTHIANS 6:14–16 NIV

. . . .

Christians are supposed to be different. We should think, act, and speak differently. Our best friendships should be among those who have made the choice to be different.

While this makes sense, it's a hard thing to follow. It's possible to find yourself really connecting with someone who has no intention of following Jesus. You can attempt to justify dating people because you believe you can lead them to Christ. This thinking puts that person above God because you've chosen disobedience to be with them.

Unless you can walk with your date toward what Jesus wants for your life, you will both ultimately walk different directions.

Dear God, You want me to be set apart. When I date, help me honor You by spending time with someone who loves You more than me. Amen.

[Jesus] died so that he could give the church to himself like a bride in all her beauty. He died so that the church could be pure and without fault, with no evil or sin or any other wrong thing in it.
EPHESIANS 5:27 NCV

. . . .

Now that you're a teen, you face whole new challenges. It's pretty hard to feel beautiful when your body is changing in ways that aren't all so glamorous. But you can have perfect beauty—all the time—through Christ. He died to make you beautiful, erasing every scar, every imperfection, every discolored mark on your body and spirit.

So while you look in the mirror and see blemishes and imperfections, God sees perfect beauty. You don't need to diet, exercise like crazy, pluck out your eyebrows, or show off your new curves to feel pretty and earn approval. You're already complete and whole because Jesus has cleansed you.

And that's something to celebrate!

Jesus, it's so hard at times to see past my image in the mirror and be happy with myself. Maybe it's because I'm looking with the world's eyes and not Your eyes. Thank You for dying for me, for covering me with Your blood and making me beautiful inside and out. Help me to see what You see and not be so concerned about the rest. Amen.

Don't worry about anything; instead, pray about everything. Tell God what you need, and thank him for all he has done. Then you will experience God's peace, which exceeds anything we can understand. His peace will guard your hearts and minds as you live in Christ Jesus.

PHILIPPIANS 4:6–7 NLT

• • • • • • • • • • • • • • • • • • •

Worry is a condition of missing faith. Worry unintentionally says you don't believe God can handle the difficulties you face. Prayer is the intentional refusal to give worry an opportunity to convince you to make it your superhero power.

If you're struggling with something or someone, give up on worry. It'll never change the outcome of the time you've invested. Thank God in advance for taking care of things.

An exceedingly wonderful peace is your gift for making a worry deposit with God. You don't have to worry about it, and He won't worry about it. He'll just take care of it.

How often should you worry? Never! When should you stop worrying? Right now! How can you stop worrying? Pray! When can you pray? Right now!

Dear God, You say I should tell You what I need, so I'm here to say I need to stop worrying. I need faith enough to trust that You've got this. Help me hold on to Your gift of peace by refusing to worry. Amen.

"But when you fast, comb your hair and wash your face. Then no one will notice that you are fasting, except your Father, who knows what you do in private. And your Father, who sees everything, will reward you."
MATTHEW 6:17–18 NLT

• • • • • • • • • • • • • • • • • •

Fasting is God's idea, but it may be unfamiliar to you. Most biblical fasting is an intentional refusal to eat for a while. Fasting isn't a diet, but a discipline that gives us more time to focus on our relationship with God. We give up something in order to gain something better.

While most people think of food when they think of fasting, there are other ways to fast. You might take a break from something you really love in order to get closer to God. That could be sports, music, or even social media.

When you need to take a break, a fast may bring life back into focus.

Act normally; a fast isn't something you do to be noticed, but something you do to notice God.

Dear God, You told us that fasting is something that honors You. Maybe a fast from the drama of the Internet can help me turn online drama into time with You. Help me also spend more time with trusted Christian friends and find new opportunities to serve. Amen.

What matters is not your outer appearance—the styling of your hair, the jewelry you wear, the cut of your clothes—but your inner disposition. Cultivate inner beauty, the gentle, gracious kind that God delights in.
1 PETER 3:3-6 MSG

. . . .

Is modesty just a girl thing? Is lust just a guy thing? In the twenty-first century we see the need for males and females to be modest and free of lust.

Lust should never be confused with love. Where love is giving and kind, lust takes and is demanding. Where love wants the best for others, lust is only interested in what it wants.

Modesty is seeing yourself as valuable enough not to intentionally reveal things that are not meant for others. Modesty also is an act of humility.

The Bible tells us that we can get so caught up in our looks that we neglect our heart. We can also get so caught up in looking at others that we can't think straight.

Inner beauty may take longer to notice, but for Christians it is true beauty that's been enhanced by God's character and love. This is a beauty worth finding.

Dear God, help me understand that what I wear and how I act affects others in positive or negative ways. Keep my eyes and heart focused on You. Keep my mind and imagination on Your plans for me. May I dress in a way that doesn't intentionally draw attention to me. May You find joy in my choices. Amen.

You should know that your body is a temple for the Holy Spirit who is in you. You have received the Holy Spirit from God. So you do not belong to yourselves, because you were bought by God for a price. So honor God with your bodies.
1 CORINTHIANS 6:19-20 NCV

• • • • • • • • • • • • • • • • • •

We hear a lot about honoring God in how we act—what we say and do. And we spend a lot of time focusing on our behavior and molding it to be more like Christ. But we also need to honor God with our bodies. When we surrender our lives to Christ, we also surrender our bodies.

So how do we honor God with our bodies? We honor Him in the way we dress—modestly and not flaunting our body parts to the world. We honor Him by eating healthy and getting regular exercise. And we honor Him by not engaging in destructive habits—smoking, drugs, eating disorders, premarital sex, cutting, etc.

How do you struggle most with honoring God with your body? What changes do you need to make in your life? How can you make those changes, starting today?

Father God, I know my body is a temple for You. Help me to respect my body and treat it in a way that is honoring to You. Please give me the strength and perseverance to make necessary changes. Amen.

A New Wardrobe

*Therefore, as God's chosen people, holy and dearly loved,
clothe yourselves with compassion, kindness, humility,
gentleness and patience. Bear with each other
and forgive one another if any of you has a grievance
against someone. Forgive as the Lord forgave you.*
COLOSSIANS 3:12–13 NIV

If you love to shop, there are a few things to add to
your list of *must-haves*. The Bible says we need to keep
compassion, kindness, humility, gentleness, and patience
within easy reach. If you're fresh out of these essentials
just get in touch with God and place an order.

God asks us to forgive, love, and be patient with
others. That's hard to do when your first options are
revenge, indifference, pride, cruelty, and irritation. As
Christians we're new creations, God's handcrafted
people, ready for something new. That's why He gave us
a new wardrobe. Our old clothes no longer fit with the
new us.

There's actually no need to shop for things like
compassion and kindness because God already gave
them to you. The real question is—will you wear them?

*Dear God, You're reminding me that I was made for a
purpose that's greater than what others believe.
You want my outward attitude to reflect the new thing
You're doing inside me. Help me cooperate. Amen.*

Don't Be a Bad Actor

If anyone boasts, "I love God," and goes right on hating
his brother or sister, thinking nothing of it, he is a liar.
If he won't love the person he can see, how can he
love the God he can't see? The command we have
from Christ is blunt: Loving God includes loving
people. You've got to love both.
1 JOHN 4:20–21 MSG

. . . .

It's easy to see the value in loving God. It's also easy to believe people are too messed up to love. When we fail to love people, we're refusing to follow God's second greatest command. Jesus said we should love God above all and then love everyone else (see Mark 12:30-31).

A hypocrite was an ancient actor. These were people who wore masks to disguise how they really felt. The masks represented something that wasn't true. It was meant to deceive, but being classic entertainment, the audience had them figured out—the stage was filled with hypocrites. They represented an illusion.

When we say we love God, but don't love people, we're like bad actors that can't fool anyone and never really look like the God we say we love.

Good news—even hypocrites can change.

Dear God, help me to be authentic. That means I admit
to You that it's hard to love other people. With Your help
I'll do what You've asked me to do and be who
You want me to be. Amen.

*Be friendly with everyone. Don't be proud
and feel that you are smarter than others.
Make friends with ordinary people.*
ROMANS 12:16 CEV

. . . .

Ashlee was my best friend in middle school, but soon the pull of the popular crowd put a strain on our friendship. She wanted to join the popular girls—and I didn't. Eventually our choices led us in different directions, and our friendship dissolved. Her popular friends dictated who she could hang out with, and I wasn't cool enough for them.

Our senior year in high school, Ashlee apologized to me and asked if we could be friends again. Her time with the popular crowd had changed her, and not in positive ways. She wanted genuine friendships again, not the plastic, shallow relationships she'd had for the last several years. She wanted to be more than a pretty face—she wanted to be liked for who she was. And my ordinary friendship is just what she needed.

Are you friendly to everyone—to the scorned crowds, the ordinary crowds, *and* the popular crowds? Who do you have trouble loving? Why? How can you befriend that person today?

*God, I don't want to miss out on friendships just because
I can't look past someone's appearance or behavior.
Help me not to care about social status, but to offer my
friendship and Your love to everyone. Amen.*

A gentle answer turns away wrath,
but a harsh word stirs up anger.
PROVERBS 15:1 NIV

When you start a conversation, the words you use are just as important as how you say them. Phrases like, "What made you think. . ." or "If you hadn't. . ." or "That was stupid. . ." are like pouring gas on a fire. We all can become defensive if we feel like others assume we've done something wrong without listening to us first.

It could be that we're at fault, but criticism can convince us to lash out, return hurtful words, and express anger.

If we can begin conversations by being gentle, we may experience a different result. If we respond to others in kindness, we're likely to find the other person can't stay angry for long. It's hard to fight someone with negative words when the other person won't participate.

Some people like drama. Do something different. Refuse to start arguments and then refuse to let one continue. One decision brings peace while the other invites anger.

Dear God, You expect me to show love in how I
respond to others. When someone is mad at me,
I have an opportunity to respond with kindness and
respect. This is hard because it is much easier to
respond in frustration. Help me be willing to give the
answers that send anger packing. Amen.

Therefore, since we have been made right in God's
sight by faith, we have peace with God because
of what Jesus Christ our Lord has done for us.
ROMANS 5:1 NLT

• • • • • • • • • • • • • • • • • • • •

Olympic training standards are very high. God's standards are even higher—He demands perfection. If you dishonor your parents, cheat, or lie—even once— He considers any one of these offenses the same as breaking all of His laws.

You could argue that your sin wasn't nearly as bad as something like murder, but God looks at all sin the same way. One sin equals total guilt.

We couldn't save ourselves, which is why it's so important that Jesus came to earth. He was the only perfect sacrifice acceptable to God. He willingly sacrificed Himself to pay the penalty for our choice to sin.

After Jesus rose from the dead we were invited to become part of God's family. God accepted the sacrifice of His Son, Jesus, so there was no longer a reason for God to declare us guilty (see Romans 8:1).

Dear God, Your Son, Jesus, made us right in Your sight.
I want to show gratitude by obeying You so I can
become more like You. When I fail, You will forgive,
but I think if You could make the choice for me,
it would be obedience—every time. Amen.

*God means what he says. What he says goes.
His powerful Word is sharp as a surgeon's scalpel,
cutting through everything, whether doubt or defense,
laying us open to listen and obey. Nothing and no one
is impervious to God's Word. We can't get
away from it—no matter what.*
HEBREWS 4:12–13 MSG

. . . .

When a company makes a cell phone, they develop an owner's manual or guide to help new users learn the benefits and limitations of the device. The same is true for cars, dishwashers, and lawn mowers. It's uncommon for someone to argue that the company really didn't understand what they were talking about when developing the manual.

God's Word is *His* word. He inspired the writing of the Bible, and it contains truth about the Maker of everything known and unknown. The Bible should receive more respect than any other owner's manual because it contains *God's* plan, truth, and life.

Even those who don't believe the truth of God's Word can't get away from what's written. It's almost as if God gave each of us a heart that will always keep looking for the truth only God offers.

Dear God, give me a hunger to know what You've said in Your Word. Help me think about Your words enough that they find a place in my heart and mind and make their way into my conversations with others. Thanks for never leaving me in the dark. Amen.

Always be joyful. Pray continually, and give thanks whatever happens. That is what God wants for you in Christ Jesus.
1 THESSALONIANS 5:16–18 NCV

• • • • • • • • • • • • • • • • • •

Ever start your day off in a bad mood? You don't want to go to school. You don't want to stay for practice. And you wish your siblings would just leave you alone. All you want is your comfy clothes, the couch, some TV, and a good dose of chocolate.

We've all had days like this. You wake up tired or cranky, and it takes all the mental energy you have just to roll out of bed and face the day. You snarl your way through breakfast, grumpily head to school, and plop yourself in your seat for first period. You don't want to talk. You don't want to take notes. You. Just. Want. To. Go. Home.

In moments like this, dig deep and find something to be thankful for. Maybe your hair cooperated today, when it usually doesn't, or you scored higher on your quiz than you expected. Focusing on the good things—and thanking God for them—will help you navigate the times when life is hard.

Lord, I'm cranky. And while I feel like life is pretty disappointing at the moment, I do recognize the little flowers of goodness around me. Thank You for those bright spots, and help me to focus on the good things as I muck my way through this rough day. Amen.

Nature's Testimony

*For ever since the world was created,
people have seen the earth and sky.
Through everything God made, they can clearly
see his invisible qualities—his eternal power and
divine nature. So they have no excuse
for not knowing God.*
ROMANS 1:20 NLT

. . . .

All of creation testifies to the nature of God. To get to know God, we read the Bible and pray and go to church and do all the normal stuff Christians are "supposed" to do. But have you ever reflected on nature and what it shows you about God?

Try it! What does a sunset tell you about God? Sunsets show me that God has an artistic nature. He loves color and variety. He is a master artist that likes to paint the sky. Sunsets also reveal to me the faithfulness of God. The sun rises and sets—every day, without fail. He is steady. He is faithful. We can always count on Him.

What do you learn about God from nature? What does grass teach you? Trees, flowers, ants? The ocean, mountains, prairies? Lions, cows, and dogs? As you go about your day, take time to observe the nature around you and contemplate what invisible qualities it reveals to you about God.

God, it's so amazing to think You've hidden a piece of Yourself in every part of creation. Open my eyes to see You in the nature around me. Amen.

Body Image

*Don't you realize that your body is the temple of the Holy
Spirit, who lives in you and was given to you by God?
You do not belong to yourself, for God bought you with a
high price. So you must honor God with your body.*
1 CORINTHIANS 6:19–20 NLT

• • • • • • • • • • • • • • • • • •

When we think about body image, we often consider
things we believe are lacking or the wrong size. We
obsess about proportions, strength, and whether people
like the way we look.

From God's perspective body image means
something much different. Our bodies won't last forever.
We'll be in heaven one day, and God wants to prepare us
now for what life will be like there.

The Holy Spirit is another of God's great gifts. Jesus
calls Him our Helper. He warns us when we consider bad
choices.

God calls our bodies the temple of the Holy Spirit,
so what we do with our bodies either keeps His house in
shape or makes it less livable.

Body image shouldn't be about how we or anyone
else views what's outside, but about how we treat every
part of where the Holy Spirit lives.

*Dear God, if every part of me is Yours, then I should treat
my body with respect because it's where Your Spirit lives
until I get to heaven. Help me care more about what You
think of my body and less about the opinion of others.
May my opinion about myself match Yours. Amen.*

"Honest" Failure

God can't stomach liars; he loves the company
of those who keep their word.
PROVERBS 12:22 MSG

• • • • • • • • • • • • • • • •

Keeping your word can be inconvenient. When circumstances change and it's no longer easy to fulfill our agreement, we can decide we're no longer obligated to keep our promises. This could be a promise to your mom or dad to clean your room. It could be a promise to a brother, sister, friend, or teacher. Maybe they're still waiting.

We may mean well, but our intentions don't mean much if we always seem to find a way to get out of a promise.

Keeping your word can cost more than you want to pay, but the payment will be worth it even if you don't think so immediately.

A broken promise is a nice way of saying a lie was spoken. Keeping a promise gives a greater opportunity for others to trust us. If we're reliable then closer friendships can develop, more responsibility will be offered, and we'll gain a good reputation.

Dear God, You don't want me happy just being a promise maker. Keeping my word is important for me, and it's important to You. If I am ever to be a leader, help me be faithful to provide an example of what it looks like to keep promises. You always have. Help me do the same. Amen.

Grace, Mercy, and Peace

*Grace, mercy, and peace, which come from God the
Father and from Jesus Christ—the Son of the Father—
will continue to be with us who live in truth and love.*
2 JOHN 1:3 NLT

. . . .

Can you tell the difference between mercy and
grace? See if this helps: Mercy is being forgiven when
punishment was the best you could expect. Grace is
being given the undeserved right of a child of God.

It looks like this. Imagine a young girl caught stealing
from the royal garden. Mercy is what set her free after
breaking the law. Grace is what allowed her access to
everything in the kingdom—including the garden.

Christians offer mercy by forgiving others for hurtful
behaviors. We offer a sense of grace by treating other
believers as equal children of God. We can be gracious to
those still seeking Jesus.

God offers peace along with mercy and grace. When
we know we're forgiven, and when we're sure we are
God's children, what is there to worry about? Peace is
the result of knowing God is our Father.

*Dear God, what could be better than being forgiven
and then made a part of Your family? You are amazing,
and Your gifts are incredible. Let me rest in Your peace
knowing if You can forgive and then give me a forever
home, You can take care of everything else. Amen.*

So you see, faith by itself isn't enough.
Unless it produces good deeds, it is dead and useless.
JAMES 2:17 NLT

• • • • • • • • • • • • • • • • • •

We're saved by faith—we can't earn our salvation—but good deeds are supposed to be a measuring stick for our faith? I'm confused!

It's like this: salvation is only possible through God's grace. We can't do anything on our own to be "good enough" to enter heaven. But once we *are* saved, we should naturally perform good deeds as proof of our faith and God's transforming work in our life.

Or think of it this way: you can do all the homework you want in the summer, but that homework isn't why your school accepts you in the fall. However, once school starts, teachers *do* expect you to complete your homework.

Grace and deeds work the same way. You can do all the good works you want, but they won't admit you into heaven. Only acceptance of God's grace gets you in. But once you're adopted as God's child, you're expected to do good things. Read James 2:14-18. Are your faith and good deeds out of balance? How?

Lord Jesus, please free me from feeling like I have to do good things to earn Your approval. It's such a relief to know I already have Your approval through the sacrifice of Your Son, which covers me. Help my good deeds be a reflection of Your grace in my life. Amen.

*"As for me, far be it from me that I should sin
against the LORD by failing to pray for you."*
1 SAMUEL 12:23 NIV

• • • • • • • • • • • • • • • • • • •

My best friend in high school was a Mormon. While our
beliefs seemed similar at first, the deeper I pressed, the
more I realized our faiths were very different. So I began
witnessing to her. Soon after we left for college, we had a
major falling out. She found out I had a group of friends
praying for her salvation and was seriously offended. I
laid out the Gospel one last time, but she rejected it and
cut off our friendship.

Crushed, I felt like my efforts for the past two years
had failed. I wanted to give up and walk away. But God
wouldn't lift her off my heart, so I committed to fast
and pray for her salvation. For two and a half years, I
fasted once a week and prayed for her. By God's grace,
we reconciled and became friends again. I didn't bring
up faith discussions anymore—she knew the truth. I just
prayed for her and loved her.

Seven years later, she finally accepted Christ.

Who has God placed on your heart? Pray for them,
and don't give up!

*Lord, today I pray for _____. I pray that You would
open the eyes of their hearts so they could know and
understand Your truth. Holy Spirit, may Your conviction
and presence be strongly felt in their lives. Amen.*

*Watch your tongue and keep your mouth shut,
and you will stay out of trouble.*
PROVERBS 21:23 NLT

. . . .

Some secrets you hear should be passed on to an adult. For instance, if someone tells you he is thinking of hurting himself or someone else, you should seek help.

Too often someone will ask us to keep a secret. We make a promise, but then go tell someone, reminding the next person it's confidential. That person then does the same thing, and soon everyone knows.

Secrets are meant to be private. Your friend may be trying to understand a struggle he or she is going through before deciding to trust you with the problem. However, when you let the details leak, it only convinces your friend that he or she made a mistake to trust you.

If you feel you absolutely must tell someone, make sure it's a trusted adult who can help. Passing information on to other people your own age only ruins friendships, increases frustration, and invites unwanted trouble.

Dear God, help me be a good friend. If someone needs help then I should get help. If someone just wants to talk through issues then I should keep my mouth shut. I can always talk to You about any problem. May I use my mouth to ask for Your help in every situation. Amen.

*Moses said to the Lord, "Oh, my Lord, I am not eloquent,
either in the past or since you have spoken to your
servant, but I am slow of speech and of tongue."
Then the Lord said to him, "Who has made man's mouth?
Who makes him mute, or deaf, or seeing, or blind?
Is it not I, the Lord? Now therefore go, and I will be
with your mouth and teach you what you shall speak."*
EXODUS 4:10–12 ESV

. . . .

Maybe you get nervous in front of people, or maybe
you sit in the crowd and can't understand why someone
would have a problem being in the spotlight.

Moses was nervous in front of people. You'd think
he'd enjoy being noticed. He grew up in the palace of the
Egyptian pharaoh, but as an adult Moses wanted to see his
family released from slavery. God sent Moses to speak to
Pharaoh. What was Moses' response? It was something like,
"Dear God, I get tongue-tied. I won't be very good at this."

Does it sound like Moses was shy? Maybe. God chose
Moses, but promised that since He made the mouth
He could help Moses with the words he needed to say.
Moses soon became something other than a shy nomad.
Moses led his people out of Egypt toward the land God
had promised them.

*Dear God, help me speak when I'm afraid.
Help me find friends in spite of my fear. You helped
Moses. Would You please help me? Amen.*

*[Jesus said,] "This is my command: Love one another
the way I loved you. This is the very best way to love.
Put your life on the line for your friends."*
JOHN 15:12–13 MSG

• • • • • • • • • • • • • • • • • •

Loving unconditionally is loving without the "ifs." The
"ifs" are the conditions we place on our gift of love. If you
love unconditionally then the other person doesn't need
to do anything but accept your gift.

Loving unconditionally isn't just something for
husbands and wives. It's true for friendships, helping
others, or visiting someone.

It seems everyone has love conditions. When you
actually do love without demands, someone might say, "I
owe you." Even they understand that most people expect
something in return. It can be hard to convince them
there's nothing to owe.

God loves us that way. We had nothing to offer God,
but He sent Jesus to love us enough to save us (see
Romans 5:6). God's love never says, "If you'll just get
your life together. If you'd just try a little harder. If you'd
just stop being something less than perfect." When we
actually accept His love, He cares enough to invite us to a
better way of living.

*Dear God, I'm grateful You love me without any "ifs."
I accept Your love, and I ask You to help me share
that love with others. May I never place demands as a
condition for really loving anyone You created. Amen.*

God's Voice

*So the LORD called a third time, and once more Samuel
got up and went to Eli. "Here I am. Did you call me?"
Then Eli realized it was the LORD who was calling
the boy. So he said to Samuel, "Go and lie down again,
and if someone calls again, say, 'Speak, LORD,
your servant is listening.' "*
1 SAMUEL 3:8–9 NLT

. . . .

"I don't know what God wants me to do!"

Finding God's direction for your life starts by
asking—and then listening. Hearing God's voice takes
practice. Even the famous prophet Samuel couldn't
recognize God's voice in the beginning! But God kept
speaking, and eventually Samuel learned to recognize His
voice.

It's hard to listen when we pray. But don't give up!
God will keep speaking until you learn to hear Him.
Sometimes He'll speak to our inner spirit, sometimes His
direction comes through scripture or wise counsel from
others, and sometimes we'll know His will through open
and closed doors or a strong sense of peace. The more
you practice listening to God, the more you will hear Him.
So get going, girlfriend!

*Lord, help me to distinguish Your voice from other voices
and know when You're speaking to me. I'm so glad
You keep speaking until I finally hear You. What do
You want to say to me right now? Amen.*

Remember your leaders who taught you the word of God. Think of all the good that has come from their lives, and follow the example of their faith.
HEBREWS 13:7 NLT

• • • • • • • • • • • • • • • • • • •

We all need inspiration and encouragement at times. When you're jogging in gym class, sometimes it's your friend running beside you that gives you the motivation to keep going and cross the finish line. When you participate in an athletic competition, it's the cheers and whistles of your coach and family members that push you to perform your best. The same is true of our faith. Sometimes we need encouragement and inspiration from more mature believers to help us keep pursuing God.

Whose walk with God really inspires you? Who do you observe and think, "Man, I want to be like that"? How have you seen God work in that person's life, and how does that challenge or encourage your own relationship with Him?

Role models don't have to be actual people you know. Pick up a biography of a well-known Christian like Corrie ten Boom, Amy Carmichael, or Rachel Scott, and let her life story inspire and challenge you.

The more you surround yourself with mature believers and their testimonies, the more you'll want to grow and see God in your own life.

God, thanks for the role models You've placed in my life. I'm so amazed at their faith and how You've worked in their lives! Thanks for their inspiration when I need encouragement. Amen.

People who work hard sleep well, whether they eat little or much. But the rich seldom get a good night's sleep.
ECCLESIASTES 5:12 NLT

. . . .

"I'm so *bored*!" you moan.

"Then find something to do," says your mom.

Sound familiar? God designed us to work. He created Adam and Eve and placed them in the Garden of Eden to tend it. He never meant for us to have a life of laziness and leisure. When you work hard, even if it's not fun, you end the day feeling satisfied and sleep well. But when you sleep all day and lounge around doing nothing—you often have a hard time going to sleep at night.

Rest and leisure aren't bad things—God even commands us to have a day of rest each week. But too much rest leads to laziness, which is definitely a bad thing (see Proverbs 10:4, 26; 12:24; 13:4; 21:25).

The next time boredom hits, examine your life. Why are you bored? Have you had too much leisure time and you're left feeling restless, lazy, and unproductive? Find some work to do, whether it's a job, helping out around the house, volunteering somewhere, or participating in a physical activity. Get moving, and you'll be a lot happier—and less bored—person!

Lord, when I'm bored, doing some kind of work is usually the last thing I want to do. Help me learn the value of work—and to have a good attitude about it. Amen.

If we claim that we're free of sin, we're only fooling ourselves. A claim like that is errant nonsense. On the other hand, if we admit our sins—make a clean breast of them—he won't let us down; he'll be true to himself. He'll forgive our sins and purge us of all wrongdoing. If we claim that we've never sinned, we out-and-out contradict God—make a liar out of him. A claim like that only shows off our ignorance of God.
1 John 1:8–10 MSG

• • • • • • • • • • • • • • • • • •

Some people have a problem saying the words, "I'm sorry." They may realize they've offended someone, but ignore the issue and try to avoid making the mistake again. That approach won't work with God. His forgiveness comes when we admit we've sinned.

God wants us to understand when we've made wrong choices. He wants us to agree with Him that His forgiveness is necessary. If we never say we're sorry, we're hanging out with pride, and that never brings us close to God.

We need forgiveness. We can't just try to do better next time. Sin requires that we acknowledge we're lawbreakers in need of forgiveness. Because we sin we need to admit the truth and accept the love of a forgiving God.

Dear God, it's no fun to come to You and admit I've blown it—again. Yet that's what You want. Help me to be honest about my actions and return to You every time I run away. Amen.

Faith is the confidence that what we hope for will actually happen; it gives us assurance about things we cannot see.

HEBREWS 11:1 NLT

. . . .

We all have doubts. Sometimes we question whether good things will ever happen. We doubt that someone who said they'd be there for us will really show up. We live in a continual state of "I'll believe it when I see it." These are perfect conditions for a hard heart with jaded expectations. You can easily believe it's normal for other people to let you down, that there is nothing you can really trust, and there's very little to look forward to.

Faith is deciding to believe all the good things that God promised before they actually happen. It's easier to make this decision because God has already kept so many promises. He has proven He's more than trustworthy, His Son gave His life to reclaim you from a past recognized for your sin choices, and He has a future that is beyond awesome.

With God, faith means you can be certain that He will do what He said He would do.

Dear God, I can't respond well to You when my heart is hard. You can't help me grow when I can't trust You. Help me find the places in Your Word where I can discover proof of the promises You've kept. Help me remember Your answers to prayer—time after time. Amen.

*Don't be naive. There are difficult times ahead. As the
end approaches, people are going to be self-absorbed,
money-hungry, self-promoting, stuck-up, profane,
contemptuous of parents, crude, coarse, dog-eat-dog,
unbending, slanderers, impulsively wild, savage,
cynical, treacherous, ruthless, bloated windbags,
addicted to lust, and allergic to God. They'll make
a show of religion, but behind the scenes they're
animals. Stay clear of these people.*
2 TIMOTHY 3:1–5 MSG

. . . .

Jesus is coming back someday. Every generation has
looked forward to His return. It seems like we're always
faced with the bad choices of people around us. That can
be a problem if we hang out with bad influences.

Take a look at the long list of choices and attitudes
common even among those who say they love God. They
care about themselves, their stuff, and their desires. They
don't really want what God loves. They chase whatever
amuses them at the moment.

How do we deal with people like this? First, we pray
for them and for ourselves. We can't make decisions for
other people, but we can take responsibility for our own
choices. You never have to do *anything* God has warned
against. You're always free to make the right choice.

*Dear God, help me accept responsibility
for my own actions. May my decisions
bring honor to Your name. Amen.*

When I felt my feet slipping, you came with your love and keep me steady. And when I was burdened with worries, you comforted me and made me feel secure.
PSALM 94:18–19 CEV

. . . .

Sometimes I just *freak out*. Maybe because I'm running late, or I forgot to do something, or I left behind something important—or all of the above. Sometimes I can work myself into a real tizzy. My mom is great during my freak-out moments. Her gentle hand on my shoulder and calming reassurance helps me slow down, take some deep breaths, and stay cool.

If I turn to God in my freak-out moments and pay attention, I often feel His reassuring hand on my shoulder, too. He'll remind me of His presence through a sunset, an encouraging phone call, a Bible verse, or a sense of peace. Jesus is always with us, catching our elbow when we slip, reassuring us when we're overwhelmed with worry.

When you freak out, where does God show you His hints of reassurance?

*Jesus, thanks for steadying me with Your love
and firm grip on my life when I'm freaking out.
Thanks for comforting me when I'm worried and helping
me feel secure when I feel like things are falling apart.
And thanks for making Your presence known
to me in little ways that make me smile.*

Dark Hatred Needs Light

Anyone who hates a fellow believer is still living and walking in darkness. Such a person does not know the way to go, having been blinded by the darkness.
1 JOHN 2:11 NLT

• • • • • • • • • • • • • • • • • • •

Loving people is one of God's greatest commands. Love is a choice we make to show that we follow God. When we think about loving other people, it's easy to think it just includes people who probably don't know Jesus and need to see what God's love looks like.

It's possible to hang around other Christians, see their faults, and end up hating them for their failures, mannerisms, and pride. Sometimes we don't even need to find fault to hate another Christian.

If you find yourself in this dark place, God's Word says you've turned your back on the light of Jesus. In that darkness you'll discover it's very hard to see where God wants you to go. You'll also find it hard to experience joy, peace, and satisfaction.

Christians should spend time together. Making the choice to love another Christ follower may be a key to your own spiritual health. It'll definitely improve your vision.

Dear God, You're not a God of hatred, but love. That love isn't just for those who need to know Your Son, but those who already do. Help me love my Christian family even when they get on my nerves. Amen.

*You want what you don't have, so you scheme
and kill to get it. You are jealous of what others have,
but you can't get it, so you fight and wage war to take
it away from them. Yet you don't have what you want
because you don't ask God for it.*
JAMES 4:2 NLT

. . . .

All abuse is the result of people not getting what they
want. They might want access to a better job, higher
grades, or nicer car, and when they don't get it they take
out their frustration on someone who may have had no
impact on the decision.

The one being abused may never understand the
reasons behind the behavior. He or she may even assume
responsibility for the abuse. Never believe it.

All abusers want their own way. They don't talk to
God because they know their ambitions don't line up
with His plan. With God there is no applause for abuse.

*Dear God, I don't want to be selfish. If wanting my
own way means I am more likely to hurt other people,
then I need to desire Your way more than any plan
of my own. Help me always choose
love over violence. Amen.*

"If you are faithful in little things, you will be faithful in large ones. But if you are dishonest in little things, you won't be honest with greater responsibilities."
LUKE 16:10 NLT

• • • • • • • • • • • • • • • • • •

"I don't know why they don't trust me."

Have you ever thought that before? You believe you can handle greater responsibilities, but all you get are ones that someone much younger could do without a problem. You think you're much too old for such minor responsibilities.

God is clear. If you refuse to take care of small things, then you shouldn't expect anyone to give you big responsibility.

It can seem humiliating to feel like you should be doing more grown-up jobs, but you're treated like you're still in preschool.

The quickest way to move forward is to make sure you *always* do the jobs that you're asked to do—even when they seem below your ability. This is what faithfulness looks like. It's more than just one-time obedience. Make it a life pattern and watch the opinions of others change when it comes to your ability—and responsibility.

Dear God, You want me to be reliable, dependable, and responsible. Help me do what I'm asked, when I'm asked, without being asked twice. I'm moving closer to adulthood every day. Please shape me into the person I was always meant to be. Amen.

*"You'll not likely go wrong here if you keep
remembering that our Master said, 'You're far
happier giving than getting.' "*
ACTS 20:35 MSG

• • • • • • • • • • • • • • • • • • • •

She puts money in the offering at church, keeping
a separate stash of cash available to help those she
sees in need. Her friends think that's unusual, but
she understands something they're still learning. She
will remember the grateful face of the young mother
who had been a few dollars short on her grocery bill,
struggling with what essential item was less critical. She'll
remember the joy of stepping in to help. She'll remember
her decision to obey.

You may not make a lot of money. You might get
an allowance and consider every dime something
you can use to buy whatever you want. But when you
intentionally give some of it away you will discover what
she did—there's incredible joy in allowing God to do
something impressive with His money.

God has given us everything we own. He doesn't
need our money to keep things in good shape. Our
giving is something that connects our heart to His. We
give because He gave. Our generosity is a sign that we
understand His heart.

*Dear God, You want me to be generous. I wouldn't have
anything if it weren't for You. Help me release my grip
on Your money and share whenever You ask. Thanks for
always being generous with me. Amen.*

Here's how you tell the difference between God's children and the Devil's children: The one who won't practice righteous ways isn't from God, nor is the one who won't love brother or sister. A simple test.
1 John 3:9 msg

• • • • • • • • • • • • • • • • • •

God wants us to judge. This isn't judging as to whether God could love, save, or accept an individual. This is a type of judgment that looks a bit like the work of a detective and less like a judge. The Bible calls this *discernment*.

Discernment helps distinguish the difference between good and bad decisions, who'd provide a good influence and who wouldn't, and who follows God and who pretends.

Today's verse can be used to become better discernment detectives. It's an easy pass/fail test. If a person makes it a practice to live according to God's Word and loves other Christians, then they represent God's children. If they don't care what God has to say and they always find fault with other Christians, then it's possible they aren't God's children.

You will never be the final judge on anyone's life—that's God's job—but discernment can help you identify who might be a trustworthy influence.

Dear God, You hate it when I'm judgmental, but You encourage me to discern between good things and bad, positive and negative influences, and things that shine Your light or bring darkness. Help me determine what influences please You and discern what to allow into my life. Amen.

Do not offer the parts of your body to serve sin,
as things to be used in doing evil. Instead,
offer yourselves to God as people who have died
and now live. Offer the parts of your body to God
to be used in doing good.
ROMANS 6:13 NCV

. . . .

Have you made the commitment to remain a virgin until you're married? If so, that's great! But purity goes much deeper than just saving sex for marriage. What about *all* of your body? Have you set boundaries for yourself to honor God not just with your whole body, but with each part?

Start with your eyes. Are you gazing lustfully at other bodies? Reading sensual material? Greedily watching make-out or sex scenes on TV?

What about your ears? Are you listening to worldly advice about dating—that it's okay to have a boyfriend, even if your parents have forbidden dating? Is listening to worldly advice making you resent your parents for their rules?

Think about your hands. Are they roaming places they shouldn't?

Lastly, consider your lips. Are they staying pure? Are you saving your kisses, or are your lips getting you into deeper physical territory than you're prepared for?

Decide now what boundaries you'll set in place to honor God with all your body parts to stay pure for marriage.

Lord, I want to be pure for my husband. Help me make wise choices now so I can have no regrets later. Amen.

"No one will be able to stand against you as long as you live. For I will be with you as I was with Moses. I will not fail you or abandon you. Be strong and courageous, for you are the one who will lead these people to possess all the land I swore to their ancestors I would give them."
JOSHUA 1:5-6 NLT

• • • • • • • • • • • • • • • • • • •

A water park near my home has several high dives. I always wanted to jump from the highest one, but one look over the edge had me scurrying back down the steps. No matter how much I psyched myself up, I could never make the jump. Then one day my dad took my hand and said he'd jump with me. I was still freaked out, but jumping with Dad gave me extra courage.

After Moses died, God gave Joshua the huge task of leading Israel to claim the Promised Land. That meant ousting a lot of nations! Numerous times God reassured Joshua that He would not abandon him and to be strong and courageous.

Sometimes God asks us to do scary things. But He doesn't leave us to jump alone. He takes our hand and plunges right in with us.

God, thank You for never abandoning me. Help me to be courageous and do the tasks You ask of me, knowing You're right there with me the whole time. Amen.

Better to be poor and honest than to be dishonest and rich.
PROVERBS 28:6 NLT

• • • • • • • • • • • • • • • • • •

Watch enough movies and you might be tempted to believe that the only way to get ahead in life is to look for loopholes, lie on applications, and take advantage of technicalities. You'd almost think people *expect* you to cheat in order to reach your goals. Honesty seems to be a foreign concept.

God looks at cheating as a dishonest way to reach a goal. He says He would rather you remain poor and retain integrity than to get rich by cheating. Even if no one ever finds out, God knows, and He'd still rather see your integrity intact than for you to rely on deception.

To cheat on a test doesn't reflect your real knowledge of a subject. To cheat on an application doesn't demonstrate your real experience and skills. To cheat during a game doesn't show your real athletic ability.

A lifestyle of cheating deprives you of ever really answering the questions related to your true capabilities. You will always be deceiving others. You'll always be deceiving yourself. Suddenly being poor and honest looks pretty good.

Dear God, You love honesty and despise cheating. You can and do forgive cheating, but You want me to use honesty in my decision-making, in my interaction with others, and in my relationship with You. Help me view cheating as a poor substitute for right living. Amen.

[God said to Job] "Who shut up the sea behind doors when it burst forth from the womb, when I made the clouds its garment and wrapped it in thick darkness, when I fixed limits for it and set its doors and bars in place, when I said, 'This far you may come and no farther; here is where your proud waves halt'?"
JOB 38:8–11 NIV

. . . .

God brings order to chaos. Maybe this is why when someone finally accepts His gift of rescue they see that life with God makes sense.

He sets ocean boundaries. He gives each season three months. He tells day and night when to start. We feel safe when we know those boundaries are set. It would seem strange for the sun to start shining at night, winter to show up in summer, or the ocean to suddenly change locations.

Christians exist with boundaries, too. When we follow God's limits on our actions we can feel as if God doesn't want us to have any fun. The boundaries help us learn God's expectations so we're free to do what we were made to do.

Dear God, You created birds to fly, not swim. You made snakes to slither, not gallop. You made me to follow You, not live apart from You. Help me recognize boundaries are for my good, not to stop me from enjoying good things. Amen.

You who are younger must accept the authority of the elders. And all of you, dress yourselves in humility as you relate to one another, for "God opposes the proud but gives grace to the humble."
1 PETER 5:5 NLT

. . . .

Some adults are quick to say, "Kids get to a certain age and think they know everything." It's true; some do. Hopefully that doesn't describe you.

God wants people like you to learn from people who've lived a bit longer. When you do, you can hear some great stories, but you'll also learn some mistakes to avoid, virtues to pursue, and a few answers to questions you didn't know you had.

Never walk around feeling superior to people who are part of a generation you don't understand. They really were once your age, and they've lived through more learning than you have. What they know may be important to learn.

When you think you know everything, you can be sure there's a new and extremely hard lesson coming that you didn't even know you needed.

Demonstrate honor and humility. Be someone who's teachable. The lessons are more understandable when you have good teachers. Those teachers can become great friends.

Dear God, You don't want me to be arrogant, but You do want me to honor those who are older than me. Help me appreciate their wisdom and the time they are willing to spend teaching me. Amen.

The LORD is close to the brokenhearted;
he rescues those whose spirits are crushed.
PSALM 34:18 NLT

. . . .

Grief feels like someone threw a boulder at your heart. Grief makes you think crazy thoughts and insists things will get worse. Grief lies to you. It holds you hostage in a place of despair and pain.

It's natural to feel grief when someone dies, after a breakup, and when you leave good friends.

Grief creates an atmosphere of loneliness. Your melancholy mood tells others it's not time to get close, but to stay away. It may not be the message you intend, but it's how others respond.

God has a special message for those who grieve. He says, "I'm here to rescue you from this horrible place." While not His exact words, the truth is the same. God knows you'll need Him when grieving. He knows you need rescue when your heart is crushed. He never leaves you to go through it alone, although some people refuse His company.

Never believe there's no way out of the grief you feel. God can, does, and will walk with you through what may feel like the "shadow of death" (see Psalm 23).

Dear God, Your heart understands grief. You gave Your only Son to rescue me. You watched Him die. You heard Him ask why You'd forsaken Him. Yet in every grief there is new potential for joy. Walk with me when I hurt the most. Thank You for understanding. Amen.

God does not show favoritism.
ROMANS 2:11 NLT

. . . .

What if God suggested that the only people He could really love had to have a certain foot size, be able to yodel, and love oregano more than any other herb? That would leave a lot of people unloved.

God doesn't show favoritism—but we do.

We'll only like people with similar interests, looks, and skin color, while others are dismissed before we know their names.

Favoritism leads to cliques, clubs, and gangs. If you're one of the favored few, you can become a part of something that is considered elite—by the favored few.

Popular people are often popular only because a small number of people said they were. The rest just go along with it.

What if you just loved getting to know people? What if someone that seems different from you helped you learn something you didn't know before? What if you were surprised by a friendship that grew from someone you'd never thought of as a potential friend?

All people need to know God, but if we get into the habit of only talking to people that fit our qualifications, then we can't share what we know with the most people.

God doesn't show favoritism. Why should we?

Dear God, it's no fun being on the outside looking in. Help me be in the inside reaching out. Help me always remember You love everybody even when they don't accept it yet. Amen.

And Jesus grew in wisdom and stature,
and in favor with God and man.
LUKE 2:52 NIV

• • • • • • • • • • • • • • • • •

We don't know anything specific about Jesus when he was a teenager, but Luke 2:52 gives us a brief summary. As Jesus grew from boyhood to manhood, we know he grew in wisdom (mentally), stature (physically), and in favor with God (spiritually) and men (socially). He lived a balanced life.

How do you measure up in these areas? Are you applying yourself at school and completing your homework? Are you eating healthy and participating in regular physical activity? Are you consistently spending time with God and growing in your relationship with Him? How about relationships with others? Do you initiate social activities with others or sit and wait to be called? Are you meeting new people or stuck in a clique?

As you examine each of these four areas, how do you need to bring better balance in your life? Are you favoring one or two areas over the others? Has one area totally fallen off your radar? Pick an area that most needs work in your life and set some goals to help you grow. Involve a parent or friend in your goals so they can help hold you accountable.

Jesus, I know You were perfect and it's impossible to be just like You when You were a teenager. But help me to follow Your example and push myself to grow mentally, physically, spiritually, and socially. Amen.

Wait for the LORD; be strong and take heart
and wait for the LORD.
PSALM 27:14 NIV

. . . .

Puberty can be rough. Boys used to be icky, but now suddenly they're attractive. Your body is changing and filling out—and maybe suddenly you're receiving a lot of male attention that never happened before. You're more and more curious about kissing. And you naturally like boys and want to be liked in return.

You hear a lot about the dating game and setting up healthy boundaries as you explore these new feelings. But what about the waiting game—your period of singleness as you wait for the right person God has for you? Do you have a strategy for waiting?

Moaning and complaining and feeling lonely aren't the most productive feelings. They only make you feel worse about being single. So how can you use this time productively? How can you *embrace* this time of waiting?

God often uses periods of waiting to prepare us for what's ahead. How do you still need to grow and mature to be a girl worth pursuing? How's your temper? Your patience? Your whining and complaining? Your attitude? Are you selfish? How thoughtful are you of others?

Instead of feeling like a reject because you don't have a boyfriend, get your waiting game on! Use this time to grow spiritually and become beautiful from the inside out.

Lord, help me to wait patiently for the right guy
and grow in You as I wait. Amen.

Labeling Others

[Jesus said,] "Don't pick on people, jump on their failures, criticize their faults—unless, of course, you want the same treatment. That critical spirit has a way of boomeranging."
MATTHEW 7:1–2 MSG

• • • • • • • • • • • • • • • • •

Discernment raises warning flags while being judgmental assumes you know enough about a situation that you can say something is true when you really have no idea.

We can decide that we want to be helpful by pointing out every flaw we see in someone. While we feel we're being helpful, we actually distance ourselves from others. God is their judge. What they need is a friend. Pray for them, love them, and if you discern there are issues to avoid, then avoid them.

Stand back and watch God work. He's done this before.

Dear God, You gave us the cure for a judgmental attitude. Really love people. Your love has a way of helping me accept people in spite of faults. May I allow You to work without my less-than-expert opinion. Amen.

He was despised and rejected—a man of sorrows,
acquainted with deepest grief.
ISAIAH 53:3 NLT

. . . .

Each person has something they really want in life. It's simple, really. They want to be accepted. They want to be loved.

However, rejection always brings its two best friends—sorrow and grief. These traits cause us to hold back and refuse to interact with others because we're afraid that the cycle of rejection will happen all over again, so we risk loneliness in an effort to stop rejection.

We're never happy when we're rejected, and somehow we assume that any rejection is God's way of saying we don't matter.

We miss all the evidence that proves something else. God loved us enough to send His Son to rescue us from sin. He cared enough about us to make a way for us to be His friends. He saw something special in us that allowed Him to offer a hope for our future. We are not rejected by God. We are loved. We are accepted. We are His family.

Dear God, You have always accepted me. You made me
and knew who I would become. Your commands shape
me into who You want me to be, and You love me.
You never reject me from coming to You.
Thanks for being patient. Amen.

"The thief comes only to steal and kill and destroy; I have come that they may have life, and have it to the full."
JOHN 10:10 NIV

• • • • • • • • • • • • • • • • • •

Do you think you're valuable to anyone? We each have a seed of insecurity inside that grows up and bears fruit when we don't want it to. It's like a voice whispers, "Hey, you're still not good enough." This voice is the thief who wants to destroy our lives. Our enemy doesn't want what's good for us. He may tempt us with small changes in thinking, or he might attempt to convince us we aren't worth anything.

We should be willing to recognize that we're insecure in our thinking, but totally secure in God's love and grace.

God came to bring us a full life. He came prepared to bless us with all kinds of spiritual blessings. We find all the security we need in being His child. All our failures mean very little when compared to knowing Him and accepting the security of His love.

Dear God, there are times when I want to know if I really have value to anyone. Your words say that You created me, love me, and have a future for me. I'm accepted by You. Help me live in the joy of Your acceptance. Help me thrive in the hope of Your promises. Amen.

*Give thanks in all circumstances; for this is the will
of God in Christ Jesus for you.*
1 THESSALONIANS 5:18 ESV

. . . .

When you were little your parents often prompted you to
say the right things with phrases like, "What do you say?"
or "Wasn't that nice?" when someone gave you a gift or
did something unexpected.

You may have hidden behind your mom or mumbled,
"Thanks" without ever really understanding gratitude.

We don't always feel grateful until we realize the
thoughtfulness that comes with every gift.

God wants gratitude to be a gift we give on all
occasions. When someone shows hospitality, holds a
door, or offers cold water on a hot day, the best gift we
can offer is thankfulness.

Even when we don't feel as if everything is going the
way we want, we should offer gratitude because things
could always be worse.

When we show gratitude, we recognize the value in
others, reject personal selfishness, and inspire growth in
relationships.

There was a reason your parents asked you to say
thanks. By understanding that gratitude is something you
give to others, you can begin to see how many gratitude
gifts you need to offer.

*Dear God, You rescued me, and I'm grateful. You gave
peace, mercy, forgiveness, and love. You are giving me
daily opportunities to show gratitude. Thank You. Amen.*

We're blasted by anger and swamped by rage,
but who can survive jealousy?
PROVERBS 27:4 MSG

• • • • • • • • • • • • • • • • •

Anger is visible and harsh, rage is anger in action, and jealousy is more dangerous than both.

Jealousy is anger and rage mixed with greed, control issues, and a bit of selfish ambition to keep it focused on what it desires most.

Jealousy leads people to physically hurt and even kill others. Jealousy is never satisfied if someone has what it wants. Jealousy is blind, bold, and bitter. It has trouble seeing the logical end of its rage.

Jealousy hangs out with hate and plots deeds God repeatedly warns against. Each wears armor that resists kindness and love and will punish those who offer these gifts.

Jealousy is a monster that can't stand wisdom, won't heed warnings, and has a faulty memory.

"Where jealousy and selfish ambition exist, there will be disorder and every vile practice" (James 3:16 ESV).

What will jealousy always keep out of its circle of friends? Satisfaction, peace, trust, forgiveness, and love. It can't entertain these guests without rethinking its existence.

Dear God, I'm at war within my own heart when it comes
to following You. I can trust You to show me the way
through feelings of jealousy or be led by an enemy that
wants to destroy me. Help me put aside jealousy
so I can hear You. Amen.

Finding Balance

Do not look out only for yourselves.
Look out for the good of others also.
1 CORINTHIANS 10:24 NCV

. . . .

Have you ever tried to ride a teeter-totter alone? You can't even get off the ground! Or have you ever ridden with someone that is way lighter or heavier than you? You still can't get off the ground, or maybe you're the one stuck in the air! To be any fun, teeter-totters require mutual weight and the pushing of each person.

Relationships work the same way. Each person needs to pull her mutual weight in a gentle balance of give-and-take. When you're the only one giving, you burn out fast and the relationship doesn't get off the ground, no matter how hard you try.

I had a friendship in high school that was out of balance. We always had to spend the night at *her* house. We always did what *she* wanted to do. And I acted like it was okay that she went to prom with the guy *I* liked. Our relationship didn't last because it was unhealthy. I was doing all the giving without receiving much in return.

Examine your friendships. How are you giving and receiving? How can you bring balance to the unhealthy relationships in your life?

Lord, please help me be a better friend where I'm
slacking on my end, and help me try to address issues
with friends where I'm pulling most of the weight.
May Your wisdom guide me. Amen.

*Now is the time to get rid of anger, rage, malicious
behavior, slander, and dirty language.*
COLOSSIANS 3:8 NLT

• • • • • • • • • • • • • • • • •

Our words make an impact. You remember the old
saying about sticks and stones? They can hurt a person,
but words never do. This may be easy to say, but much
harder to believe. Because we've all faced insecurity; the
words others say about us impacts our emotions and
heart in a way a slap on the face can't.

Some believe what we say and how we say it is less
important than allowing others to see Jesus in our lives.
When we let a string of profanity flow from our lips that's
strong enough to melt the screen on our cell phone,
we leave people with a belief that what we say and do
doesn't match who we say we are.

Because we represent Jesus, our words should sound
different from what's expected. In place of criticism
we speak the language of encouragement. Instead of
profanity we speak blessing. Instead of gossip we speak
love.

If we do that, we'll speak words others will want to
hear.

*Dear God, when my words are formed in anger,
rage, malicious behavior, and slander, they will be
so emotionally driven that they won't form thoughts
that represent You. No wonder You ask me
to get rid of these traits. Amen.*

Do No Harm

I plead with you to give your bodies to God because of all he has done for you. Let them be a living and holy sacrifice—the kind he will find acceptable. This is truly the way to worship him.
ROMANS 12:1 NLT

. . . .

God gives you an amazing number of choices. You can follow His commands or choose to reject them. When you choose to reject them, that choice can show up in embarrassing ways.

Your mouth can bless or curse. Your hands can promote peace or war. Your feet can follow God or run away. Your body can be an acceptable gift to God to use as He wants or a personal experiment that could harm your body and testimony. This applies to what we drink, eat, touch, smell, and look at. It also applies to what we put into our body without concern for what it does to our thinking or actions.

The Bible says we worship God when we dedicate our body to the things He wants for us. His commands are for our safety and benefit, but they are also because, in our obedience, others may notice God for the first time.

Dear God, may I never allow anything to come between me and the honor of Your name. Help me avoid those things that take me down any path that doesn't include You. Amen.

The Lord has heard my plea;
the Lord will answer my prayer.
Psalm 6:9 nlt

· · · · · · · · · · · · · · · ·

When I was fifteen, I made a plea to the Lord. "Please, *please*, God, protect my heart. Don't let me give it away until I meet the right guy."

I was deathly afraid of falling in love only to get my heart broken. And falling in love again to have my heart broken again. So I earnestly prayed that God would guard my heart and I'd only fall in love one time—with my future husband.

God definitely answered! When guys were interested in me, I wasn't interested in them. When I really, *really* wanted to date a guy, that guy just wanted to be friends. But the real test came in college: A guy wanted to date me, and after much prayer, I felt God saying it was okay to date him. "The green light! This must be it!" I thought. "He's going to be the one!" But he wasn't. Several months later, we ended the relationship and parted as good friends. Nothing messy. No hurt feelings.

In that moment, I realized God not only protected my heart by keeping me *out of* relationships, but He also protected me *in* relationships. He had my heart, and He wasn't letting go until the time was right!

Lord, please guard my heart. I place it in Your
hands. Please keep it safe, and don't release it
until the right time. Amen.

There are "friends" who destroy each other, but a real friend sticks closer than a brother.
PROVERBS 18:24 NLT

* * * * * * * * * * * * * * * * * *

Have you ever noticed how much drama there is on social media? Pictures feature negative comments. Posts are criticized. Sarcasm flows like the Mississippi River at flood stage. You log off the computer feeling like you've just witnessed a violent crime. Maybe you participated.

Many adopt a personality that's different than their own when they post online. They post hurtful things they'd never be bold enough to say in person.

Social media isn't better or worse than TV, video gaming, or smartphones. However, there are many who are more than willing to continue the spread of bad conduct online.

We've all seen the "friends" who destroy each other. Instead, be a friend that sticks closer than a brother. Decide before you go online what you'll participate in, accept, pass along, and laugh at.

Don't be afraid to step away for a while. Ask your family for help if there's an issue you don't know how to handle. Spend time with God. He's always willing to interact with you—even when the power is out.

Dear God, help me know when to shut off social media. I never want to be one who hurts others through the words I use online. Help me remember anything I post is a reflection of my relationship with You. Amen.

*We are instructed to turn from godless living
and sinful pleasures. We should live in this evil world
with wisdom, righteousness, and devotion to God.*
TITUS 2:12 NLT

• • • • • • • • • • • • • • • • • •

Flirting is usually viewed as a way to let someone of the opposite sex know you like them. The root word of *flirting* can be defined as "without meaning." Perhaps the reason for this is flirting rarely leads to long-term, healthy relationships.

Girls who flirt are often thought of as without virtue. When guys flirt they are often indicating they have no real interest in a lasting relationship. They just want to spend time with girls.

The Bible calls this cycle godless living and sinful pleasure. God wants us to turn away from this path. Selfishness is at the core of flirting. The one who flirts is seeking his or her own interests and often cares little about the one with whom he or she is flirting.

Philippians 2:3 says, "Don't be selfish; don't try to impress others" (NLT). Does this sound anything like flirting to you?

Flirting can also lead you to entertain thoughts you might not usually think and cause you to lust. Flirting can indicate you have an interest in a physical relationship that's always to be saved for marriage.

*Dear God, flirting doesn't show others that I want to honor
You. It doesn't show that I really love others the way You
do. Help me honor You in every relationship. Amen.*

Being Different

*But Daniel was determined not to defile himself by eating
the food and wine given to them by the king.
He asked the chief of staff for permission not
to eat these unacceptable foods.*
DANIEL 1:8 NLT

. . . .

When Babylon captured Jerusalem, Daniel found himself
as a slave in a foreign country. Suddenly outside of his
religious comfort zone, he made a decision. Daniel was
determined not to let the culture around him define
what was acceptable for him. That meant firmly holding
to his beliefs and finding creative solutions to get
around cultural practices. Instead of accepting his plate
of assigned food, Daniel asked permission to eat only
vegetables and drink water instead of consuming the
unclean meat and wine (see vv. 11–14).

Following Jesus will always mean living differently
than the world around us. The world does not and should
not define our standards and boundaries. Only Jesus
should be our guide. What pressures do you feel from
the crowd? What decisions do you need to make in your
heart? How can you creatively stand your ground without
being rude or obnoxious?

*Lord, sometimes it's so hard to be different. It's much
easier to go with the flow. But I know You want me to
do what's right, no matter what others think. Help me to
stand my ground and follow You, no matter what. Amen.*

*"Study this Book of Instruction continually.
Meditate on it day and night so you will be sure to obey
everything written in it. Only then will you prosper
and succeed in all you do."*
JOSHUA 1:8 NLT

* * * * * * * * * * * * * * * * * *

Homework. . .ugh! It's such a pain, especially when you can spend your time doing more fun activities. Sure, you might enjoy doing math homework or English homework, if that's your thing, but no one enjoys doing homework from *every* subject. You discipline yourself to do it anyway because if you don't do your homework, you fail your classes. And if you fail your classes. . .you have to repeat your grade. No one wants to be stuck in the same grade again instead of advancing forward!

Our spiritual life is much the same way. If you want to prosper and succeed, you have to put in the work. When you study God's Word, spend time talking with Him, and stretch yourself to obey what He wants you to do, you'll advance into a deeper, fuller relationship with Him. But if you neglect your spiritual life to spend your time doing more fun things, you'll stay stuck where you are.

Does your relationship with God feel a little lacking? Buckle down and do some spiritual homework and see where it takes you!

*Lord, help me to continually study Your Word
and obey You so I can keep growing
and not get stuck where I am. Amen.*

*Lazy people irritate their employers, like vinegar
to the teeth or smoke in the eyes.*
PROVERBS 10:26 NLT

• • • • • • • • • • • • • • • • • • • •

My grandma lamented that it's hard to find good workers
among kids my age. She told me how babysitters in her
day helped moms by doing dishes or sweeping floors or
picking up toys in addition to watching the kids. "You be
a good worker," she said. "Moms need help. Always be
looking for how you can bless others and do more than is
required."

I took her advice to heart, and from that day forward,
I always included washing dishes and picking up the
house as part of my babysitting duties. Moms were
so thankful and so blessed. Not only did I gain regular
babysitting gigs, but I felt great serving parents who
were worn out and really appreciated a helping hand.

How's your work ethic? When you babysit, do you
just sit on the couch and watch TV? Or do you keep the
TV off, interact with the kids, and clean the house after
the kids are down?

Do you view each job as a chance to bless others, or
as a total drag, only doing the bare minimum?

Be a girl worth hiring! Work hard, and you'll be
rewarded.

*Lord, help me not to be lazy and irritating to the people
who hire me or the people I'm serving. Help me be a
good worker who blesses others and serves them like
You would serve them. Amen.*

Take care that you are not carried away with the error of lawless people and lose your own stability. But grow in the grace and knowledge of our Lord and Savior Jesus Christ.
2 PETER 3:17–18 ESV

. . . .

Relying on emotions to determine truth is dangerous. Sometimes very likable people can convince you to believe something that's not true simply because their friendship means too much to you.

Our enemy, Satan, does the same thing. He can make things look really impressive. We can be tempted to believe a lie when our emotions convince us we're looking at truth.

One statement that's been around for years is, "How could it be wrong when it *feels* so right?" God cares less about your feelings and more about your obedience.

We're flooded with issues that appeal to our emotions. It can be easy to throw common sense away in favor of beliefs that can never be supported by God's Word.

God wants stability in our lives. When we chase after the latest issues with only emotions to guide us, we shouldn't be surprised when we find ourselves off track.

Dear God, You want me to manage my emotions so I'm not unstable in what I accept as truth. Whenever I need to know truth, help me seek Your Word in spite of how I feel. Amen.

God created man in his own image, in the image of God
he created him; male and female he created them.
GENESIS 1:27 ESV

• • • • • • • • • • • • • • • • •

God created the first man. When He saw it was not good
for man to be without companionship, He created the
first woman. These two were designed to complement
each other in every way, and it was good.

At some point you'll grow up, leave home, and fall
in love. If you're obedient, you will save yourself for
marriage. God calls you to sexual purity for the physical
union of husband and wife.

Casual sex takes something meant for your future
spouse and gives it to one or many.

Inappropriate touching causes your mind to entertain
sexual thoughts that should be reserved for marriage.

God's design for marriage is one man and one
woman who have saved their sexuality to give to each
other on their wedding night (see 1 Corinthians 6:18).

Sex is a good idea created by God. It's a gift for
those who are married to enjoy. It's also something that
allows children to be born into a family.

Waiting is necessary so you can enjoy God's best
plan for you.

Dear God, help me accept that there are things I
shouldn't fully understand about sex until I'm married.
Help me accept that the mystery is worth the wait.
Help me trust that Your plan for me
is incredible. Amen.

You know well enough from your own experience that
there are some acts of so-called freedom that destroy
freedom. Offer yourselves to sin, for instance,
and it's your last free act. But offer yourselves to
the ways of God and the freedom never quits.
ROMANS 6:16 MSG

. . . .

Habits bring freedom or slavery, life or death, satisfaction
or discontentment. Some habits start early and last a
lifetime. Others can result from the devastating pressure
of others.

Some people have no interest in helping you achieve
God's plan. If other people know you want to follow God,
they may consider it an achievement to see you stumble.
Once you go back on your word to God, it can be hard
to return. God forgives, but wants you to turn away from
sin. It's hard to see God when you're too ashamed to look
His direction.

Habits form when you refuse to admit you're wrong.
This spiritual baggage gets harder to carry with each
passing day.

Dear God, no matter how many times I fail,
help me turn back to You immediately. Help me seek
You immediately when I make bad choices. Amen.

*Remember your Creator in the days of your youth,
before the days of trouble come and the years approach
when you will say, "I find no pleasure in them."*
ECCLESIASTES 12:1 NIV

• • • • • • • • • • • • • • • • • • •

The teen years are full of promise. You can't wait to
drive and have your own car. You look ahead to your
future with excitement and imagine the adventure and
independence of college. Your future is a blank canvas,
and you can be anything or do anything you want!

What most teens *don't* realize is how your choices
now can drastically affect your future. One simple choice
now can have consequences for the rest of your life that
you never imagined. Ask a teen mom how bright her
future looks. Or a high school senior who drove drunk
and killed someone in a car accident. Many teens and
college students who live the wild life while they are
young come to regret it when they're older.

But if you remember your Creator and stay
committed to Him now, you're setting yourself up for
success—both now and later! Instead of looking back
with regrets and feeling like you've wasted parts of your
life, you can look back with peace and happiness and feel
abundantly blessed at all the Lord has given you.

The choice is yours—starting now.

*God, help me to make wise choices so I don't have
any regrets when I'm older. I want to be committed
to You and not dabble in the empty pleasures
of the world. Amen.*

Honor God by accepting each other,
as Christ has accepted you.
ROMANS 15:7 CEV

. . . .

Kristi was the new girl in school, and everyone was abuzz about her. I immediately pegged her as a snob and disliked her. Even when my brother started dating her, I refused to befriend her. She started coming to youth group with us, and I finally got to know her (begrudgingly!). But the more time I spent with her, the more I realized I'd misjudged her. She was shy, not snobby. And really nice. We became good friends and are still friends today.

It's super easy to make snap judgments about people and write them off or not want to include them. But God wants us to accept each other, just as He has accepted us. Ethnicity, gender, popularity, athletic ability, beauty, and socioeconomic status aren't concerns to God, so they shouldn't be concerns to us.

What judgments have you made about people you don't really know? Do you avoid befriending people who aren't part of your crowd? Ditch the clique! You could be missing out on some really great lifelong friendships.

Lord, please forgive me for making snap judgments
about people. You look past our faults and accept us.
Help me to be open and accepting of others and to reach
out in friendship today to someone I usually avoid. Amen.

The temptations in your life are no different from what others experience. And God is faithful. He will not allow the temptation to be more than you can stand. When you are tempted, he will show you a way out so that you can endure.
1 CORINTHIANS 10:13 NLT

• • • • • • • • • • • • • • • • • • •

There's a big difference between temptation and trials. Many think they're the same. The first gives you a choice, but both give you an opportunity to trust God deeply.

Our enemy, Satan, uses temptations to try to convince us we don't really have to follow God's instructions. He wants us to fail. When we do fail, he's quick to suggest that God could never love someone who sins. He's lying.

Trials are struggles that seem too big to handle. This might be the loss of a job or home. It could be an impossible health issue.

God's Word says He gives us everything we need to resist temptation. We endure by following His instructions.

The same is never promised for trials. So next time you hear that God doesn't give you anything you can't handle, remember that He actually does. Sometimes the only one who can rescue us from the trials we face is God. If we could do it ourselves, we wouldn't need Him.

Dear God, You've equipped me to resist temptation.
You can rescue me from the most difficult trials
I'll face. You've given gifts that can't be bought.
You must really love me. Thanks. Amen.

*We demolish arguments and every pretension that sets
itself up against the knowledge of God, and we take
captive every thought to make it obedient to Christ.
And we will be ready to punish every act of
disobedience, once your obedience is complete.*
2 CORINTHIANS 10:5–6 NIV

* * * * * * * * * * * * * * * *

Can you explain to others the reason you follow God? If
someone asks you a question about your faith, could you
answer?

There are a lot of confusing ideas out there, and no
one seems willing to say there is an absolute truth. Most
people will say something like, "You can't tell me what
to believe." That's true, you can't. However, their lack
of belief doesn't change the fact that Jesus said, "I am
the way and the truth and the life. No one comes to the
Father except through me" (John 14:6 NIV).

*Dear God, You want me to discern whether what I hear
is true when compared to the Bible or if it's something I
should abandon with a warning to others. Help me listen
to others, share what I know, and match their claims
against Your Word. Amen.*

How Long?

How long must I struggle with anguish in my soul,
with sorrow in my heart every day?
PSALM 13:2 NLT

. . . .

There's not much that feels worse than being alone. This
isn't the spending-time-by-yourself alone, but the kind
that believes no one cares enough about you to even
think about you. This is the type of alone that not only
collects negative thoughts, but rejects hope.

The book of Psalms showcases brilliant moments of
worship, but also painful moments where the writer feels
rejected and completely alone.

These verses in God's Word are intentional. We get
a front row seat to some incredible pain. The writer talks
about enemies, setbacks, and profound loneliness. A
phrase that occurs throughout Psalms is, "How long?"
The writer feels like the pain will never end. He wants
hope, but hope is rare.

There are those who may think death is a good way
to end the loneliness. If this ever crosses your mind,
remember that when a Psalm starts with "How long?" it
continues by pointing to the hope found in the God who
can answer the question.

Dear God, I never face struggles alone. You know the
way through and out of the loneliness I feel.
When I need help, let me find it. When I need hope,
let me always look to You. Amen.

Mean people spread mean gossip;
their words smart and burn.
PROVERBS 16:27 MSG

· · · · · · · · · · · · · · · · · ·

It doesn't take much effort to say something about someone that you have no proof is true. You could make it up or tell others something you heard.

If you wanted to know how lightbulbs were invented, you could make up a story or ask around and get a *maybe-that's-true story*. Here's a creative idea: Why not go to a qualified source to get your information? You might feel a little awkward if you've been telling people that a guy named Jimmy discovered the lightbulb hovering over him when he had his first good idea.

If that sounds ridiculous, so is gossip, and God tells us not to do it.

Gossip is a sin, and it's not a smaller sin in God's eyes than lying, cheating, stealing, or murder.

Even if the only sin ever committed was gossip, we'd still need the perfect sacrifice of Jesus to pay the price. Every sin is a big deal. God's forgiveness is a bigger deal. Obedience is our best response.

Dear God, there are a lot of things I should skip talking
about. When I share stories that I've not been given
permission to discuss, then I'm essentially finding
opportunity to point out the faults of others when
I have no idea if what I'm saying is true.
Help me stop the gossip. Amen.

*"Always remember these commands I give you today. . . .
Talk about them when you sit at home and walk along
the road, when you lie down and when you get up.
Write them down and tie them to your hands
as a sign. Tie them on your forehead to remind you,
and write them on your doors and gates."*
DEUTERONOMY 6:6–9 NCV

• • • • • • • • • • • • • • • • • •

I'm a huge fan of sticky notes! If I need a reminder about
something important, I jot it on a note and post it where
I'll see it—the bathroom mirror, the refrigerator, beside
my bed, on my steering wheel, or even on the coffeepot.
I'm literally surrounded by sticky notes.

Visible reminders are really great tools for helping us
keep focused on what's important. That's why God told
the Israelites to keep His commands by putting visual
reminders in places they'd see frequently. You can do the
same by writing scripture on notecards and posting them
in your locker, around your mirror, on your wall in your
bedroom, or even beside the toilet (a great time to take
a minute to pray or meditate). So grab some notecards
and get started today!

*Father, I'm so thankful for Your Word and all the
guidance, encouragement, and comfort it brings me.
As I place scripture in visual places all around me,
help me to feel Your presence all day long. Amen.*

Later, when Peter came to Antioch, I had a face-to-face confrontation with him because he was clearly out of line. Here's the situation. Earlier. . .Peter regularly ate with the non-Jews. But when that conservative group came from Jerusalem, he cautiously pulled back and put as much distance as he could manage between himself and his non-Jewish friends. That's how fearful he was of the conservative Jewish clique that's been pushing the old system of circumcision.
GALATIANS 2:11–13 MSG

. . . .

My friend Katie loved hanging out with us—until someone more popular came around. Then she'd ditch us. One minute she'd be all buddy-buddy, and the next instant she'd act like she didn't know us. We finally confronted her about it, and she tearfully apologized. She had fallen into the trap of thinking she was better than us and given in to peer pressure so the popular girls would accept her.

Even Peter—Jesus' own disciple!—fell into the same trap. One minute he was befriending non-Jews, and the next he was ditching them like he didn't know them because of pressure from the conservative Jewish crowd.

Do you treat people differently when different crowds are around? Would Jesus?

Jesus, help me treat everyone the same—no matter who is around. And give me the courage to confront friends when pressure from cliques causes them to mistreat or ignore others. Amen.

*An eye that disdains a father and despises a mother—
that eye will be plucked out by wild vultures
and consumed by young eagles.*
PROVERBS 30:17 MSG

. . . .

Sometimes God teaches lessons through word pictures. Today's verse offers a look at the end result of rebellion. What we see suggests that God takes rebellion seriously.

One of the problems with rebellion is it never seems to stop with the sin of rebellion, which can easily exist with dishonor, anger, selfish ambition, pride, and impatience.

Our families are given to us to help us learn to make good choices. When we insist on being rebellious instead of obedient, our parents may become less interested in guiding us. Stop listening and your family may stop speaking. The sad news is you will always wind up losing when rebellion becomes your typical response.

Rebellion always leads to regret. Admit the sin, accept God's forgiveness, apologize for your words and actions, and find a place to retire both a rebellious heart as well as the list of regrets that always stand ready to accuse.

Dear God, I should ask for Your help when I feel like rebelling. I don't want to live with regrets, so help me honor those You tell me to honor. May I resist rebelling against my family. Amen.

The Stubborn, Stony Sin Heart

[God said,] "I will give you a new heart, and I will put a new spirit in you. I will take out your stony, stubborn heart and give you a tender, responsive heart."
EZEKIEL 36:26 NLT

• • • • • • • • • • • • • • • • • •

Work with a shovel and your hands will become hard and rough. Play a guitar and your fingers develop a thicker layer of skin so they don't hurt when playing. This is a picture of what it's like to live with ongoing sin choices.

When you sin long enough, your heart develops a thick covering, making it less interested in God's plan. Imagine what that spiritual heart looks like after many years. Scars are evident along with dark and hard patches where sin has pounded away at principle and hope. This is the type of heart God is talking about.

This is the stubborn, stony sin heart that God can replace with a tender and responsive heart. It's true. God offers a spiritual heart replacement. This happens when we accept Jesus, but the potential of a newly hardened heart is something every Christian faces.

Maybe you understand what a hard heart looks like. Maybe it's time for something new.

Dear God, I want to respond to You in the right way. Some days I'm not sure I can. A hard heart makes it difficult to take anything seriously. I want to be responsive, and I need Your help. Amen.

Finding Treasure

Every part of Scripture is God-breathed and useful one way or another—showing us truth, exposing our rebellion, correcting our mistakes, training us to live God's way. Through the Word we are put together and shaped up for the tasks God has for us.
2 Timothy 3:16–17 MSG

. . . .

When we say that the Bible is *inerrant,* it means the Bible contains no errors. God inspired men over many centuries and locations to write His words. The Bible wasn't written in a single language or through one person. The Bible is a book of history and has been used to locate important artifacts. It is a book of poetry. Psalms represents this writing style perfectly. It contains love stories, battles, miracles, and instructions for living.

Seeing God's words in printed form is like finding treasure. We don't have to guess what God wants from us. We don't have to wonder what He provides for us. We can read that the God of the universe identifies with us, loves us, and has a plan for us.

We can trust His words, which are "God-breathed and useful. . . showing us truth. . .correcting our mistakes. . .[and] training us to live God's way."

We have His words. There's treasure here.

Dear God, thank You for never leaving me without direction. I have Your words and Your Spirit to help me learn and understand the many things You want me to know about You and the life You want me to live. Amen.

*For God so loved the world, that he gave his only Son,
that whoever believes in him should not perish but have
eternal life. For God did not send his Son into the world
to condemn the world, but in order that the
world might be saved through him.*

JOHN 3:16–17 ESV

• • • • • • • • • • • • • • • • •

God loves you. Salvation through His Son, Jesus, is the
greatest gift humankind will ever know.

We may all be familiar with John 3:16, but it's the
next verse that helps us understand that God is the
inventor of grace. He could have sent each of us a list
of law violations with a threat of what might happen to
us if we don't change. He could have developed a huge
prison system for lawbreakers (although all of us have
broken His law—see Romans 3:23). He could even have
destroyed the earth and started all over again. He could
have, but He chose grace instead.

Verse 17 tells us that God didn't use the plan of
salvation to initiate a secret agenda to condemn us.

It's easier to love someone who is for us—not
against us.

*Dear God, You provided an atmosphere
where I could identify with Jesus, trust Him to
take care of me, and view Him as worth following.
Salvation is a free gift. The only thing I have to do
is trust (believe) in who You are and what You
can do. Thanks for accepting me. Amen.*

I have stored up your word in my heart,
that I might not sin against you.
PSALM 119:11 ESV

• • • • • • • • • • • • • • • • • •

Before there were banks or credit unions there were coffee cans and piggy banks. People would place coins and dollars inside and make a withdrawal when their need was the greatest. It was a pretty sad day when there was a need, but no money stored up.

When you take the time to memorize a Bible verse, you're intentionally storing it away for a future need. The more you *fill up* your memory bank the easier it'll be to make a withdrawal.

Memorizing God's Word helps us remember what He's said even when we're not near a Bible. Knowing His Word means it's less likely we'll question what God has said. We can use our internal hard drive to access God's truth so we can handle temptation, share God's truth anywhere, and remember the words when we need encouragement.

We don't memorize to earn gold stars, but to develop a sense of awe at who God is.

Dear God, You want me to store Your Words on
the pages of my heart. Please help me make regular
memory deposits filled with Your truth. Amen.

This is love: that we walk in obedience to his commands.
As you have heard from the beginning,
his command is that you walk in love.
2 JOHN 1:6 NIV

• • • • • • • • • • • • • • • • • •

In the Old Testament there are dozens of laws. The most famous have been called the Ten Commandments (see Exodus 20). In the New Testament Jesus said the two greatest commandments had to do with how we love God and how we love others (see Mark 12:28–31).

If we're transformed from people who choose sin to people who choose God's plan through obedience then we probably need to understand how we get from one choice to the other.

Obedience is simply choosing to love. If we really love someone, we won't lie to them, steal from them, or say rude things to or about them. If we love God, we'll honor His name, take Him seriously, and serve Him well.

We're transformed when our choices are defined by love (see 1 Corinthians 13).

Our journey with God begins with multiple steps of loving obedience and ends with a transformation in the way we act, think, and live.

Dear God, You give me every opportunity to obey.
You give me all kinds of ways to be obedient through
choices to love others. Help me start remembering that
obedience is a transformation from mistrust to love. Amen.

*Many even among the leaders believed in him.
But because of the Pharisees they would not openly
acknowledge their faith for fear they would be put
out of the synagogue; for they loved human
praise more than praise from God.*
JOHN 12:42–43 NIV

• • • • • • • • • • • • • • • • • • •

I recently made some new friends who aren't Christians, and I found myself hiding my faith, afraid of their reaction once they learned I was a Christian. Would they still accept me? Or would they distance themselves from me, treating me like an outsider, judging me? So I kept quiet. But I couldn't hide my faith forever—it's too much a part of me. More importantly, I didn't want to. Whatever their reaction, I wanted to be true to myself and God.

Do you ever hide your faith because you fear people's reactions? Are you afraid your friends will make fun of you? Jesus endured humiliation to die for you. Will a certain group ostracize you? Jesus left heaven so you could be with Him. Do you crave the crowd's acceptance? More than anyone, Jesus—the Creator of the universe—wants you to be His friend.

Jesus is not ashamed of you. Don't be ashamed of Him.

*Jesus, forgive me for the times I've denied You or hidden
my faith from others because I feared their reaction.
Help me share my faith openly and honestly. Amen.*

*"For a child is born to us, a son is given to us.
The government will rest on his shoulders. And he will
be called: Wonderful Counselor, Mighty God, Everlasting
Father, Prince of Peace. His government and its peace
will never end. He will rule with fairness and justice
from the throne of his ancestor David for all eternity."*
ISAIAH 9:6–7 NLT

• • • • • • • • • • • • • • • • • • •

Bombs are launched from one nation to another. Crime in our communities plasters the local news. Feuding parents lead to divorce and broken families. All around us, there's so much pain and suffering and injustice. People try to promote peace, but can it really happen? With Jesus—yes!

Jesus came to establish peace—not only with Him, but with each other. Acceptance of His sacrifice on the cross brings peace between us and God. And following His ways promotes peace with those around us by forgiving, loving, and serving one another. Whether warring nations or warring parents disrupt our lives, the Prince of Peace has the power to bring harmony.

What personal or global situations need your prayers for peace today?

God, sometimes peace seems so impossible. The hate is too strong. The hurt is too much. But You are the God of the impossible. Please bring Your peace today. Amen.

How can you claim to have faith in our glorious Lord
Jesus Christ if you favor some people over others?
JAMES 2:1 NIV

• • • • • • • • • • • • • • • • • •

When Mandy joined our mission trip team, I groaned
inwardly. Mandy came from a poor family so she dressed
in old, shabby clothes. Zits covered her face and her
teeth were yellow. She also had the most obnoxious
laugh, and talked *constantly*. Basically—she annoyed me!
I avoided sitting by her, often turned my back on her to
engage in conversation with other people, and tried to
interact with her as little as possible.

But during our mission trip, I discovered her
wonderful spirit. She loved freely and easily. She was
kind and thoughtful, meeting needs of others quickly and
unselfishly.

I learned an important lesson from Mandy. Never play
favorites! You never know what someone else's faith can
teach you.

God, forgive me for favoring some people over others.
Help me to see people like You do and treat
everyone fairly and with respect. Amen.

*"Peace I leave with you; my peace I give you.
I do not give to you as the world gives. Do not let
your hearts be troubled and do not be afraid."*
JOHN 14:27 NIV

• • • • • • • • • • • • • • • • • • •

Horatio Spafford famously wrote the hymn "It Is Well with My Soul." But do you know his story? A thriving lawyer in Chicago, he had wealth and prominence. But a series of tragedies stripped him of everything. His only son died of scarlet fever at the age of four. A year later, the Great Chicago Fire wiped out the city and all of Horatio's wealth. Two years later, all four of his remaining children died in a shipwreck. Sailing for England to join his wife, who survived the shipwreck, he passed the spot where his daughters were buried at sea. Upon seeing the sight, Horatio sat down and penned "It Is Well with My Soul." All his children—gone. His house—burned. But His soul—at peace.

Even in the face of tremendous heartache, Christ's peace anchored Horatio. No matter what happens, can you also sing, "Whatever my lot, Thou hast taught me to say, It is well, it is well with my soul"? Why or why not?

*Jesus, I'm so thankful for Your peace and comfort,
especially during tough times. Death and tragedy
don't have to hurt so much because of the hope You give.
Please give me peace and comfort today for
the things that upset me. Amen.*

How gracious he will be when you cry for help! As soon as he hears, he will answer you. . . . Whether you turn to the right or to the left, your ears will hear a voice behind you, saying, "This is the way; walk in it."
Isaiah 30:19, 21 NIV

• • • • • • • • • • • • • • • • • • •

Sometimes making decisions seems like playing hide-and-seek with God. He hides—and we have to seek! But Jesus always wants you to find Him.

You won't get very far in hide-and-seek if all you do is stand in one spot. You have to search. You can pray and pray and pray when you need God's direction, but you also have to get your move on. Take some action! Move a little to the left. Rats, a closed door. Okay, how about to the right? Oh, an open one! Okay, what's through here?

If you aren't sure which summer job to accept, pursue all your options until you feel God guiding you to the right one. Unsure what spring sport to play? Try out for soccer *and* track, and see which one brings you more joy and peace.

Finding God's will shouldn't remain an unsolved mystery. The magi followed a star. Moses saw a burning bush. Elijah heard a whisper. Look around you. What clues is God giving you?

Lord, thanks for always guiding me. Help me move in the right direction by opening and closing doors and giving me peace when I make the right decision. Amen.

Being afraid of people can get you into trouble,
but if you trust the LORD, you will be safe.
PROVERBS 29:25 NCV

• • • • • • • • • • • • • • • • • • • •

Some girls on my bus asked me to write dirty notes for
them. I wanted their approval and friendship, so I agreed.
I wrote what they dictated, trying to dismiss my unease
about the sexual content. I knew what I was doing was
wrong, but I couldn't find the courage to speak up
and stop it. I didn't want to be picked on for being the
"goody-two-shoes."

Our bus driver found the notes, gave us a strong
lecture, then corralled us to the principal's office.
My parents were called, and I wanted the floor to
open up and swallow me whole. Facing my parents'
disappointment was the worst. I was so embarrassed and
ashamed of what I'd done. All because I let peer pressure
overrule what I knew God wanted me to do.

Don't get caught in the trap of peer pressure. Always
stand up for what you know God wants, and you'll stay
safe.

God, it's really hard sometimes to speak up and not get
involved with things I know are wrong. Help me take a
stand and have the courage to follow You
and what I know is right. Amen.

*All praise to God, the Father of our Lord Jesus Christ.
God is our merciful Father and the source of all comfort.
He comforts us in all our troubles so that we can comfort
others. When they are troubled, we will be able to give
them the same comfort God has given us.*
2 CORINTHIANS 1:3–4 NLT

· · · · · · · · · · · · · · · · · ·

The Bible says, "In this world you will have trouble"
(John 16:33 NIV). God promised that difficulties would be
normal. That may sound like a promise we'd be happy
to see God fail to keep. We don't like to worry, fear, or
struggle. The good news is we don't have to.

God is described as merciful. He offers comfort
whenever the struggles come. He may not shield us from
trouble, but He does give us a place to rest in the middle
of the trials we face.

In those times of testing we grow, we're stretched,
and we learn a lot about ourselves and others. When God
comforts us, it becomes our responsibility to comfort
others and help them find God, the ultimate source of
comfort.

We often ask why we have to go through difficulties,
but if we accept that everyone struggles then we may
ask the new question, "What do You want me to learn?"

*Dear God, because You love us You provide comfort.
Help me remember compassion demonstrateslove. Amen.*

Roll up your sleeves, put your mind in gear, be totally ready to receive the gift that's coming when Jesus arrives. Don't lazily slip back into those old grooves of evil, doing just what you feel like doing. You didn't know any better then; you do now. As obedient children, let yourselves be pulled into a way of life shaped by God's life, a life energetic and blazing with holiness. God said, "I am holy; you be holy."
1 PETER 1:13–16 MSG

• • • • • • • • • • • • • • • • • •

Conforming is like placing your palm on a memory foam pillow. The pillow quickly takes the shape of your hand. When you decide to stop obeying God, you can quickly take the shape of the many bad decisions you face every day. You *slip back into those old grooves of evil.*

For the Christian, there is a better way. You no longer have an excuse for making bad choices. God always offers forgiveness, but He has always wanted us to grow up. He tells us, "I am holy; you be holy."

That's wisdom from a God that knows it's easy for us to make selfish decisions.

Dear God, I need to be disciplined in my journey with You. Help me refuse to be conformed to the shape of the easy decisions around me. Help me break the mold and be used by You to reshape the culture around me. Amen.

Don't be misled: No one makes a fool of God. What a person plants, he will harvest. The person who plants selfishness, ignoring the needs of others—ignoring God!—harvests a crop of weeds. All he'll have to show for his life is weeds! But the one who plants in response to God, letting God's Spirit do the growth work in him, harvests a crop of real life, eternal life.
GALATIANS 6:7-8 MSG

• • • • • • • • • • • • • • • • • • •

If life is a farm and we're farmers, then we're in the business of growing crops. If we don't plant good seed then weeds will grow.

A good crop has a positive impact on our lives and on the lives of others. We share love, hope, and kindness, and we harvest the same.

A bad crop is defined by its negative impact. When we express anger, violence, and hatred, we shouldn't be surprised when we don't gather a crop of joy.

If you think you can play along the fringes of a bad crop grown by others, you're likely to bring back bad seeds that overtake your crop.

Let God's Spirit clean out the weeds in your life and plant new seed. A harvest is coming. What's your life producing?

Dear God, it takes time for any crop to grow, but there will come a time when everyone can see what type of seed I planted. Help me plant a crop that represents Your work in my life. Amen.

*But he was pierced for our rebellion, crushed for our
sins. He was beaten so we could be whole.
He was whipped so we could be healed.*
ISAIAH 53:5 NLT

• • • • • • • • • • • • • • • • • •

I like all kinds of movies (except horror flicks!). Action
films, chick flicks, and documentaries—I love them all! But
war movies always get under my skin. I hardly ever watch
a war film without crying. As a civilian, I frequently take
my freedom for granted and forget how many soldiers
sacrifice their lives so I can live in peace.

As a Christian, sometimes I forget how much Jesus
suffered to give me freedom and peace, too. But the
Bible offers a vivid and constant reminder of how much
Jesus suffered and sacrificed for me and for you.

Just as we honor the military and remember fallen
soldiers, don't forget the high price Jesus paid for your
spiritual freedom. Remember His sacrifice and give Him
heartfelt thanks for your salvation.

*Jesus, I'm so humbled and overcome at the sacrifice
You paid for me. Thank You for laying down Your life
for me. Thank You for saving me! Amen.*

*This means that anyone who belongs to Christ
has become a new person. The old life is gone;
a new life has begun!*
2 CORINTHIANS 5:17 NLT

· · · · · · · · · · · · · · · · · · ·

Ninety percent of sexually exploited women were abused as children and fell through the cracks of society, landing in prostitution. The US State Department estimates 100,000 children (average age thirteen) enter sex trafficking *every year*. The sex trade is a modern-day form of slavery where women and girls are turned into property to be bought and sold.

Ninety-five percent of trafficked women say they want out of their lifestyle, but they do not believe they can survive doing anything else. New Friends New Life is a Christian organization based in Dallas, Texas, that seeks to restore and empower trafficked teen girls and sexually exploited women and their children by providing access to education, job training, temporary financial assistance, and counseling. Their mission is to rehabilitate women, giving them new friends and a new life.

Learn more at www.newfriendsnewlife.org.

Thank You, Father, for organizations that seek to restore abused women and give them a new life. Please give sex victims courage to start a new life. I pray that sex victims will find true hope, healing, and salvation in You. Amen.

A Day Is Coming

Therefore, with minds that are alert and fully sober,
set your hope on the grace to be brought to you
when Jesus Christ is revealed at his coming.
1 PETER 1:13 NIV

• • • • • • • • • • • • • • • • • • •

One day Jesus will come back. He will still be the Savior, but His coming means the start of something new. Earth isn't the end of His plan. He's created a place for each Christian in the place where He lives—heaven.

What happens here is only the beginning, but it is where the greatest decision about where we will spend eternity is made.

It takes faith to believe in a God we've never seen who lives in a place we've never been, but who has always existed, always will exist, and who created our world with nothing but the words He spoke.

Yet faith means we see proof of His existence in the air that we breathe, in the sun that rose this morning, in the food we eat, in the water we drink, in the friends we make, and in the family we love.

God wants us to take our faith seriously. He wants our minds, hearts, and lives locked into following Him so when He returns we'll be found faithful.

The best life is ahead.

Dear God, You don't want me to play games with my
faith. I shouldn't look at following You as the next big
trend, fad, or trial offer. You're God. Help me always
understand the need to follow You. Amen.

Praise God in his sanctuary; praise him in his mighty heaven! Praise him for his mighty works; praise his unequaled greatness! Let everything that breathes sing praises to the LORD.
PSALM 150:1–2, 6NLT

. . . .

We're told to praise God, but what does that mean? In today's culture we usually think of a church service or outdoor festival where people sing songs to and about God. There are praise bands, praise songs, and praise gatherings, but is this all there is to praise?

Music does seem to be one of the most-used methods to praise God, but to praise means more than singing songs. To praise God can look like an awards ceremony where you think of all the reasons God deserves your trust and faith. Praise can be a bit like boasting by telling others how amazing God is. Praise can be a session of gratitude where you thank God personally for the many gifts He has given.

Dear God, when I praise You, I'm letting You know I understand You made everything, gave everything, and deserve everything I've got—and I agree that You're more than worthy of all the gratitude I can ever give. You're beyond awesome. Amen.

Living in Harmony

*Each one of you is part of the body of Christ,
and you were chosen to live together in peace.
So let the peace that comes from Christ control
your thoughts. And be grateful.*
COLOSSIANS 3:15 CEV

. . . .

My roommate and I did *not* get along during my
freshman year of college. She liked to stay up late; I went
to bed early. She liked music and lots of noise; I preferred
quiet. She was messy; I was neat. Our differences in
lifestyle caused some serious clashes. Although we had
been close friends before college, suddenly we found
our friendship very strained. I finally prayed for God to
calm me with His peace and heal our friendship. It took
time—and lots of effort!—but we eventually resolved our
differences and lived in harmony with each other.

Sometimes it's just hard to get along, whether it's
with friends, siblings, or even parents. But God wants
us to live in unity and harmony with each other. How
hard do you strive for peace in your relationships? Or do
you just accept—and maybe cause!—the division? What
can you do today to help bring peace to your strained
relationships?

*Oh, Lord, sometimes I get so angry with my friends and
family. It is so easy to lash out at them with my words.
Help me take a deep breath and control my thoughts
with Your peace. Amen.*

*LORD, rescue me from evil people; protect me from cruel
people who make evil plans.*
PSALM 140:1–2 NCV

• • • • • • • • • • • • • • • • • •

Human sex trafficking has become *the* human rights
issue of today. According to the FBI, it's the fastest
growing business in organized crime. The majority
of sex trafficking happens in other countries, but did
you know that around 300,000 American youths are
at risk for becoming victims and an untold number
have already been taken for trafficking? Girls between
the ages of twelve and fourteen are forced into
prostitution, and even boys between the ages of eleven
and thirteen are trafficked in the United States. Victims
are sold to traffickers, locked up for weeks or months,
drugged, terrorized, and raped. Victims become so
afraid, they don't fight and they won't escape, even
when presented with an opportunity. Once they are
prostituted, the average victim is forced to have sex
twenty to forty-eight times a day.

Human trafficking isn't just an international
problem—it's a local one. Trafficking happens in all fifty
states, 365 days a year.

With your parents' permission, you can learn more
about human trafficking at www.polarisproject.org.

*Jesus, please rescue sex trafficking victims, and help
them find healing. Please help people to be aware so
trafficking can be prevented and better reported
to the authorities. Amen.*

I was becoming a leader in the Jewish religion, doing better than most other Jews of my age. I tried harder than anyone else to follow the teachings handed down by our ancestors. But God had special plans for me and set me apart for his work even before I was born. He called me through his grace and showed his son to me so that I might tell the Good News about him to those who are not Jewish.
GALATIANS 1:14–16 NCV

• • • • • • • • • • • • • • • • • •

Paul was the model Jew. He grew up memorizing scripture, attending synagogue every week, and participating in Jewish festivals. He did everything right! But one day he met Jesus face-to-face, and his whole life changed.

Many teens have the same background as Paul. They grow up in Christian homes, attending church and youth group every week, memorizing scripture, and participating in Christian holidays. But they haven't met Jesus face-to-face.

Our faith isn't just a bunch of rules and beliefs passed down from our parents and grandparents; it's a personal encounter with a living God. Have you had a life-changing experience with Jesus Christ, or are you just going through the motions, leaning on your parents' faith?

Jesus, I want to know You—truly know You. Not just learn about You and "do the right things." Please show Yourself to me so that I can know You personally and the plans You have for me. Amen.

"Whoever believes in me is really believing in the One who sent me. Whoever sees me sees the One who sent me. I have come as light into the world so that whoever believes in me would not stay in darkness. Anyone who hears my words and does not obey them, I do not judge, because I did not come to judge the world, but to save the world."
JOHN 12:44–47 NCV

• • • • • • • • • • • • • • • • • •

I don't know about you, but it's *so easy* for me to judge others.

"I don't feel sorry for her. She got what she deserved."

Gasp! "She did *what?* And she calls herself a Christian?"

"She's so fat. She totally needs to eat better and stop being so lazy."

"Look at what she's wearing! Oh my gosh. She's so immodest."

Ever have similar thoughts? We can respond to people in two ways: judge and condemn them for their behavior or extend grace and lovingly guide them to Jesus. Just as Jesus reflects the Father, we reflect Christ. And Jesus didn't come as a judge, but a redeemer.

So stop those judgmental thoughts in their tracks when they come chugging through your mind. Instead of judging people's actions, think about how you can show love and grace, shining God's light in their life.

Father, You alone know people's hearts
and situations. Help me reflect Jesus
and the love and grace He showed. Amen.

For you have been called to live in freedom,
my brothers and sisters. But don't use your freedom
to satisfy your sinful nature. Instead,
use your freedom to serve one another in love.
GALATIANS 5:13 NLT

. . . .

You are free to love. You are free to serve. You are free to be what God made you to be.

The freedom God gives isn't bent toward selfishness, but bent toward seeing freedom as a way to bless others.

Every trait that God wants to develop in our lives has the choice to love at its center. He calls this love *freedom*.

When we serve others, we're demonstrating the truth of our choice to love. After all, who serves the needs of others if they don't really care for them?

Service requires humility because you're not looking out for the things you want, but for the needs of others. Sometimes the people you serve are people you don't even know. However, when you know the individual you serve, it creates the opportunity to view others as more important than you.

Perhaps one of the greatest freedoms we have is freedom from selfishness.

Dear God, You want me to be freed from self
and free to share life with others. Help me see
freedom as never having to apologize
for serving others in Your name. Amen.

My purpose in writing is simply this: that you who believe in God's Son will know beyond the shadow of a doubt that you have eternal life, the reality and not the illusion. And how bold and free we then become in his presence, freely asking according to his will, sure that he's listening. And if we're confident that he's listening, we know that what we've asked for is as good as ours.
1 John 5:13–15 MSG

• • • • • • • • • • • • • • • • • •

God has never been a vending machine. Does that sound like an odd statement? Sometimes we treat Him as if all we need to do is pay the price of a prayer and He'll *have* to answer our request in the way we want it answered.

Since God knows everything, He's aware of what's good for us and what will cause us harm. Wouldn't God be irresponsible if He let us have things He knew would harm us?

When we invite God to fuse His will with our request, the answer we receive will be perfect. Does that mean God will give us what we want? It means we learn to desire God's will over our requests.

Dear God, help me always ask for Your best. Help me remember that when I leave the decision to You, I'll always get something much better than I planned. Amen.

*You will show me the way of life, granting me
the joy of your presence and the pleasures
of living with you forever.*
PSALM 16:11 NLT

. . . .

It's possible to think that if God is all you have then you don't really have much. Some people think it's like choosing a library over a roller coaster. They feel that God just isn't exciting enough to allow Him to influence every part of their life. What if they spend time with God and miss out on something fun?

Surrendering to God means your perspective will change. You'll discover a secret that will surprise you. Every amazing experience you've ever had won't satisfy you the way God can. Every experience has a beginning and end. You'll get tired of each new experience. God always comes through.

God invites us to really live life with Him. That life comes with joy-filled satisfaction, encouraging us to put everything else lower on our priority list. Experiences can make us happy, but only God can bring joy, and in His presence you'll always find a greater satisfaction you didn't know was possible.

Dear God, I could never have a greater life than the one I can have as Your child. Help me seek and find satisfaction in You. Help me surrender my will for Your way. Amen.

*My friends, be glad, even if you have a lot of trouble.
You know that you learn to endure by having
your faith tested. But you must learn to endure
everything, so that you will be completely
mature and not lacking in anything.*
JAMES 1:2–4 CEV

• • • • • • • • • • • • • • • • • •

Nobody *likes* to suffer. Even if you're a committed athlete, there are some days you just don't want to practice—especially if practice is so hard it makes you vomit! But we recognize that the training, the suffering, matures us—it makes us better. We're stronger and more skilled, sharper and more in control.

You can't mature into a champion athlete by sitting on the couch!

Our spiritual life is the same. A strong, committed faith in God doesn't just happen. It has to grow. God allows trouble to come into our life so that He can train us and mature our faith. The valley—not the mountaintop—is where God makes us stronger.

What struggles are you facing right now? What do you think God is teaching you? How is your faith growing?

*Lord, life is not fun right now. It actually really hurts.
It's hard to find any joy in all this, but I do find comfort
in You. I do feel You growing me. So thank You for this
experience and deepening my faith in You. Amen.*

*The Lord is a mighty tower where
his people can run for safety.*
PROVERBS 18:10 CEV

* * * * * * * * * * * * * * * * *

"Tag, you're it!"

Aw man! I hate being "it" in hide-and-seek. It's much more thrilling to dash for the safety of "home base" and elude the danger of being tagged. Even better, it's much nicer to stay on home base and be completely protected from being chased at all!

In life, Jesus is our home base, our safe zone. When we run to Him, He protects us against the powers of darkness. You don't have to run scared from evil forces that are trying to tag you—feelings of rejection, loneliness, and being unloved. Believing that you don't measure up, that you'll fail, that others don't like you. That you aren't thin enough, good enough, pretty enough.

When the Devil's lies start chasing you, run to Jesus. Ask and trust Him to protect you. Like a warrior, He'll shield you from the enemy, keeping you safe and unharmed. He'll cover you with His truth, reassure you with His love, and bolster you with His strength.

What lies chase you? How does the enemy like to tag you and drag you down? Let Jesus' power and truth wash over you, and run to Him for safety.

*Mighty God, thank You for protecting me. For being
a safe place to run when I feel the enemy chasing me.
Please shield me today from the enemy's attacks,
and help me stand strong in You. Amen.*

Consider it a sheer gift, friends, when tests and challenges come at you from all sides. You know that under pressure, your faith-life is forced into the open and shows its true colors. So don't try to get out of anything prematurely. Let it do its work so you become mature and well-developed, not deficient in any way.
JAMES 1:2–4 MSG

• • • • • • • • • • • • • • • • • • •

Have you ever thought of a bad day as a gift? What if days like this exist to provide a better picture of what's really important?

It can be easy to think that the most important thing in life is to have days without stress, worry, and pain. The trouble is we often forget God when things are good.

We live in a world where it's easy for people to make bad choices. Bad things often happen just because we live in a world where people sin. Our lives and the sin of humanity will clash from time to time. That's when we remember why God is so important.

The pressure of bad days can help us bring our faith out of hiding and prove that we really trust God.

Dear God, sometimes bad days help shift my focus back to You. When bad things happen, I remember You. That doesn't mean You make things bad so I'll notice, but today I am noticing, and I'm grateful. Amen.

*In heaven I have only you, and on this earth you are
all I want. My body and mind may fail, but you are my
strength and my choice forever.*
PSALM 73:25–26 CEV

. . . .

Your house is on fire, and you only have *one* thing you
can save from being burned to ashes—what would you
grab? No cheesy answers like your Bible or your pillow. But
seriously, what would you be absolutely devastated to lose?

The answer to this question reveals your ultimate
possessions in life. What would happen if it were
destroyed? Why is it so special? Is the value sentimental
or monetary?

Chances are what you grabbed isn't something you
could take to heaven with you. You never see a U-Haul
following a funeral procession so the person who died
can be buried with all his belongings.

So what really matters? Is it stuff? People's opinions
of us? How well we perform?

It all really boils down to God. He's our ultimate
possession—the one thing we can never lose.

What do you fear losing? What possessions do you
cling to? What status are you chasing? What do you
need to surrender to God in order for Him to be the
ultimate desire of your heart?

*God, it's so easy to chase after unimportant things.
To guard my stuff and not want to share it.
But You are what's truly lasting and most important.
I surrender everything to You. Amen.*

Blessings and cursing come pouring out of the same mouth. Surely, my brothers and sisters, this is not right! Does a spring of water bubble out with both fresh water and bitter water?
JAMES 3:10–11 NLT

• • • • • • • • • • • • • • • • •

Jeremy came from a very poor family. Because he was smelly, overweight, and obnoxious, kids always made fun of him and picked on him before youth group started. Then the youth pastor would get the night rolling, and the same mouths that had mocked Jeremy switched to praising God.

When you make fun of others, you are essentially making fun of God because we are all made in His image. When you use your words to hurt or mock others, you are hurting and mocking God. Bitter saltwater added to a glass of freshwater ruins the whole glass. Similarly, your praises to God are empty if you're speaking badly of others.

The next time you're tempted to lash out or make a biting remark, zip the lip! If you mess up and say things you shouldn't, make it right. Ask for God's forgiveness and the other person's. Use your words to be an instrument of blessing, not destruction.

God, help me honor You with my words—not just in praises, but in how I speak to others. Amen.

A tiny spark can set a great forest on fire. And among all the parts of the body, the tongue is a flame of fire...it can set your whole life on fire, for it is set on fire by hell itself.
JAMES 3:5–6 NLT

• • • • • • • • • • • • • • • • • • •

I'm short. And I can't jump. So naturally, I did not play as spiker on our community volleyball team. I played the back row and was the setter in front. But what's a volleyball practice without spiking drills? When my attempt to spike a volleyball failed horribly, my brother shouted with disgust, "April, why do you even try?"

His words sliced my self-esteem, and I still carry that scar today. Our words, though small, have the potential to spark a massive fire and damage another person. One biting remark, one off-hand comment can cause more ongoing destruction than you ever imagined. Watch your words, and speak carefully!

Lord Jesus, the tongue is so hard to control! I don't want to cut others with my words and leave lasting scars. Help me to heal from the wounds I've received, and convict me before I let loose biting words that can wound others. Amen.

*All kinds of animals, birds, reptiles and sea creatures
are being tamed and have been tamed by mankind,
but no human being can tame the tongue.
It is a restless evil, full of deadly poison.*
JAMES 3:7–8 NIV

• • • • • • • • • • • • • • • • • • •

Tongue twisters drive me nuts! My mind knows what it
should say, but my mouth pops out the wrong thing! But
with enough practice (and going slowly enough!), I can
recite tongue twisters correctly.

Taming our words can seem an impossible task.
You know what you *should* say, but out pops mean and
unkind things. But good news! We don't have to tackle
this impossible task on our own. The Holy Spirit will help
you. So pay attention to His nudges, and the more you
practice controlling your words, the easier it will become.

How much control do you use when speaking? Do
you try to filter your words, or do you just let them fly
without thought? Do you find yourself easily criticizing,
or do you like to encourage? In what way do you most
need to work on taming your tongue?

*Holy Spirit, please show me how I need to watch my
words. Convict me when I'm saying things I shouldn't,
and help me practice restraint—holding in the damaging
things I want to say. Help me not to criticize and gossip,
but to lift up and encourage. Amen.*

*If we confess our sins, he is faithful and just and will
forgive us our sins and purify us from all unrighteousness.*
1 JOHN 1:9 NIV

• • • • • • • • • • • • • • • • • •

What's your weakness? What do you give in to? What
mistake do you repeatedly make?

We all have weaknesses. We all sin. But it's our
response to sin that's key. Do you retreat from God
because you enjoy the sin so much you'd rather wallow
in it than walk away from it? Do you beat yourself up
with guilt and come up with strategies on how it's never
going to happen again? Do you hide it from the world
and act like everything is fine, but find yourself buried
with shame? Do you go out and have fun because if you
forget about it, you'll feel better?

There is never a time you'll feel more unworthy
to approach God, to sit in your shame and ask for
forgiveness, than when you make a mistake. But when
weakness wins, love prevails. God's love for you is not
dependent on who you are, what you have to offer, or
how "good" you are. God loves you. Period.

God's love is undeserved and beyond what you could
pay for it. But it's there, for you, ready and available to
experience, if you confess your sins.

*God, I've messed up—again. Please forgive me.
I feel so unworthy, so undeserving. Thank You for
revealing to me the depth of Your grace. Amen.*

Dancing with the Spirit

*Since we live by the Spirit, let us keep in step
with the Spirit. Let us not become conceited,
provoking and envying each other.*
GALATIANS 5:25–26 NIV

• • • • • • • • • • • • • • • • • • •

I love to dance! In middle school my dad surprised me
with two-stepping lessons. It's a country dance that
requires partners, so every week Dad and I had a date
and learned to two-step. Dancing with a partner is far
different than dancing solo. As girls, we have to follow
the guy's lead. When I didn't follow Dad's lead, we'd trip
and stumble over each other and mess up the dance
moves. But when I stayed in step with him, we sailed
across the dance floor doing all kinds of fun spins and
twists.

If you want to live by the Spirit, it's a lot like dancing.
You have to follow His lead. If you try to go your own
way, you'll trip and stumble through life. But if you let
the Spirit lead, seeking His guidance and listening to His
prompts in your spirit, you'll sail much more smoothly.

Are you taking charge of your life—making your own
decisions and going your own way? What's one thing
you can do today to allow the Holy Spirit to direct your
life?

*God, I want to dance beautifully with You. Help me
submit to You today and learn to do things Your way
so we dance well together. Amen.*

Repent of your sins and turn to God, so that your sins may be wiped away.
ACTS 3:19 NLT

• • • • • • • • • • • • • • • • • •

It doesn't take much skill to sin, and it only gets easier.

Doing the wrong thing can seem empowering. Wearing the wardrobe of a rebel can appear to offer independence, but it never does.

The choice to sin is actually inviting our enemy to influence future decisions.

God knows the end result of sin is death, which is why He gives us access to life.

We're restored in our relationship with God when we turn from the easy choice to sin to the life-affirming choice to obey. Repentance requires turning away from the choice to sin.

Sometimes we want to be forgiven, but we don't want to stop making the same sinful choice. We ask God to forgive, but keep looking at and entertaining the same sinful choices.

The choice to turn away can seem hard. You have an emotional attachment to sin. God wants to change your mind. Repentance is your positive response to His desire to restore you to life.

Dear God, there are times I don't want to do the right thing. You offer forgiveness, but You want me to turn my back on the easy choice and follow You. Help me listen for Your voice, read Your Words, and follow Your plan. Amen.

God as Father

"I am the Alpha and the Omega," says the Lord God,
"who is, and who was, and who is to come, the Almighty."
REVELATION 1:8 NIV

• • • • • • • • • • • • • • • • •

When we think of God as our Father, many times we naturally compare Him to our own father. But our earthly fathers aren't perfect, and that can create misperceptions about God. So what does the Bible say Father God is like?

He is the Creator of everything (see Acts 17:24–29) and the sovereign ruler of all nations (see 1 Timothy 6:15). He is a holy judge who deserves respect and reverence (see 1 Peter 1:15–17; Ephesians 2:1–3). He demands justice for our sins, but also provides loving mercy through offering His own Son to take our punishment (see Romans 3:24–26). He loves us and takes pleasure in us and lavishes us with His blessings (see Ephesians 1:3–14). He is faithful (see 1 Corinthians 1:9) and passionate about restoring our relationship with Him (see John 3:16).

What does the term *Father* mean to you? How much does your relationship with your earthly father affect your relationship with your heavenly Father? Is your view of God unbalanced? After learning what the Bible says about God as Father, how does your perception of Him need to change?

Father God, Your role as holy judge makes me approach
You with reverent respect. But Your compassion, mercy,
and love overwhelm me. You are mighty and powerful,
yet You love fervently. Thank You for loving me! Amen.

Christ is the visible image of the invisible God.
He existed before anything was created
and is supreme over all creation.
COLOSSIANS 1:15 NLT

• • • • • • • • • • • • • • • •

Praise Jesus! Without Him, we would not have a complete picture of God. As part of the Trinity, Jesus existed before creation and was fully God while also becoming fully human (see Philippians 2:6–11). But Jesus' role is different from the Father's.

While the Father is the Author of all creation, He created through Jesus and Jesus sustains all life (see John 1:3; Colossians 1:16–17; Hebrews 1:2–3). Therefore, Jesus is supreme over all creation (see Colossians 1:15, 18; Hebrews 1:6). Jesus is Emmanuel, "God with us" (see Matthew 1:23), and the forgiver of sin (see Matthew 9:2; Luke 7:48; John 3:18).

The holiness of the Father keeps Him separate from us. We cannot see His face and live (see Exodus 33:20–23). But in His grace and mercy, God sent His Son so that we may see the face of God and receive the forgiveness of our sins. God is no longer separate from us, but through Jesus (Emmanuel!) God is now among us and we can truly know Him. That is definitely worth some praise!

Jesus, You are so awesome! You created everything and sustain the workings of the universe. You became human so God could dwell among us and so we could be forgiven and restored to the Father. Thank You, God, for revealing Yourself to us. Amen.

God as Holy Spirit

*"But I will send you the Advocate—the Spirit of truth.
He will come to you from the Father
and will testify all about me."*
JOHN 15:26 NLT

• • • • • • • • • • • • • • • • •

Of all the members of the Trinity, the Holy Spirit causes the most controversy among Christians. Some completely overlook Him and minimize His power and presence. Others overemphasize the power of the Holy Spirit and place Him in a position of prominence over the Father and the Son. What does scripture say about this third member of the Trinity?

Jesus sent the Holy Spirit so we wouldn't be left as orphans when He ascended to heaven (see John 14:18). Now God is not just *with* us, but *in* us (see John 14:17; Romans 8:11; 1 Corinthians 6:19)! As our advocate, He comforts, encourages, and counsels us (see Acts 9:31; John 14:16, 15:26). When we don't know how to pray, the Holy Spirit prays for us (see Romans 8:26). He identifies us as God's children, guaranteeing our eternal salvation (see Ephesians 4:30).

Through the Holy Spirit, God's presence is with us all the time, teaching us, guiding us, convicting us, and encouraging us. Jesus revealed God to us, and now the Holy Spirit allows God to live inside us!

*Holy Spirit, thank You for never leaving me. I'm so glad
You remain in me, guiding me, counseling me,
and encouraging me. Continue to change me
and make me more like Jesus. Amen.*

Die, Suckers!

And because we belong to Christ Jesus, we have killed our selfish feelings and desires.
GALATIANS 5:24 CEV

. . . .

My *favorite* lip gloss in high school was Purple Posy (don't judge). It was a shimmery, light plum shade that looked really good on me. Apparently, my best friend thought it looked great on her, too. Because *every day* she'd ask to borrow it. And *every day* it got harder and harder to pull it out of my backpack to share it with her. Selfish thoughts raced through my mind. Mostly to the tune of, *Well, if she likes it so much, why doesn't she buy one herself instead of using all mine!*

Makeup isn't cheap, especially the good stuff. But God convicted me. Would I really be petty over a tube of lip gloss? Didn't my friendship mean more than a measly twenty bucks? And didn't my best friend share her things with me?

Sigh. All right, all right! So I killed my selfish desires that wanted to hoard my good lip gloss—*not* easy to do!—and continued to share. Because God wanted me to.

Wrestling down those selfish desires and impulses is no easy feat! But God calls us to serve each other, to give freely as He does, to not make things more important than people. What selfish feelings do you wrestle with? How can you kill them?

Lord, help me not to be selfish with my things, my time, or my attention. Amen.

*When you follow the desires of your sinful nature,
the results are very clear: hostility, quarreling,
jealousy, selfish ambition. . .and other sins like these.
But the Holy Spirit produces this kind of fruit in our
lives: love, joy, peace, patience, kindness, goodness,
faithfulness, gentleness, and self-control.*
GALATIANS 5:19–23 NLT

In this passage, Paul strongly contrasts the sinful
nature with the fruit of the Spirit. Everyone can tell the
difference between hatred and love, rage and kindness,
getting drunk and having self-control. When we become
"new creations" (2 Corinthians 5:17) in Christ, the sinful
nature should disappear more and more while the fruit
of the Spirit grows more evident. Just as the fruit of
the Spirit contrasts sharply with the deeds of the sinful
nature, Christians should stand out in the world.

Read over today's scripture again. What descriptions
from the sinful nature especially stand out to you? What
fruit of the Spirit do you see in your life? Which ones
need to become more evident?

*Ouch, God. I'm still letting my sinful self rule by
_____. Please forgive me and work in my heart
and life to be more _____. As You transform
my life, I pray that I would sharply contrast the world in
my behavior so others can see You in me. Amen.*

*If you are tired from carrying heavy burdens,
come to me and I will give you rest.*
MATTHEW 11:28 CEV

. . . .

Sometimes do you ever just feel. . .burned out? Out of gas? The homework, the practices, the social obligations, running here, running there. You just want to drop into bed, pull the covers over your head, and sleep for a whole weekend.

Feeling burned out is a good sign that you need rest—that you're carrying too much by yourself. When we're accelerating through life on our own gas, we'll quickly putter out. We need to spend time refueling with God. Even Jesus withdrew from His busy ministry to spend time resting and refueling with the Father. Luke 5:16 says, "But Jesus would often go to some place where he could be alone and pray" (CEV). Did you catch that? Jesus *often* sought time alone.

How often do you seek downtime to be alone and spiritually refreshed? If you need some gas, some pep in your step, be sure to make a pit stop and drop your burdens at Jesus' feet. He'll refill your tank and give you the strength and energy you need to face your day.

*Jesus, I'm so tired. I haven't been very good about
coming to You for encouragement and refreshment.
I spend my downtime zoning out in front of the TV or on
my phone, but that doesn't really refill my spirit. Help me
turn to You for the rest I really need. Amen.*

Each of you has been blessed with one of God's many wonderful gifts to be used in the service of others. So use your gift well.
1 PETER 4:10 CEV

. . . .

What do you love to do? Even if it exhausts you, what leaves you feeling satisfied and happy? Do you love to watch kids? Teach others? Fill a need?

If you like to babysit, moms always need help! Especially moms with young children. Why don't you offer some free babysitting? Approach a mom you know well and ask if you can bless her by giving her some time off. Maybe you can watch her kids so she can shower or run errands. Or maybe you can take her kids for a walk to the park so she can stay home and nap.

Do you like to teach? Ask about volunteering in a Sunday school class for children's church or joining the volunteers in the nursery.

Do you love to encourage others? Think of some people in your life that could really use a boost and write them an encouraging note.

God doesn't want us to be consumed with ourselves. He blesses all of us with special gifts to be used for serving others. What gifts do you have? How can you serve someone today?

God, show me what gifts You've given me and how You want me to use them to serve others. Amen.

Sacrifice of Praise

Thank the LORD because he is good.
His love continues forever.
PSALM 118:1 NCV

• • • • • • • • • • • • • • • • • •

During church, we often approach worship the same way we approach the sermon: What can I get out of it? If we don't walk away feeling spiritually encouraged and refreshed after our time of singing, we feel like the effort was a waste. But worship isn't for *us*. It's for *God*. We worship Him because He deserves our praise.

Worship is like writing thank-you notes. You don't write thank-yous to make *yourself* feel better; you write them to express honest and genuine thanks for a gift you've received. You may not feel like sitting down and writing a note, but you do anyway because the person deserves your acknowledgment and appreciation.

Some days it's easier to praise God than others. Some days we feel really close to Him, and some days offering any praise or thanks feels like it's vanishing into a void. Regardless of our feelings, we need to participate in worship and genuinely thank God for His goodness, love, and blessings in our life.

Instead of spending most of your prayer time today making requests of God, spend your time thanking Him and praising Him for who He is and for what He's done for you.

Lord, You are so good. You continually surprise me
with loving gifts, and You're so faithful to provide—
every time. I praise You for being sovereign
and wise, for being just but merciful.

Day and night your hand of discipline was heavy on me. My strength evaporated like water in the summer heat. Finally, I confessed all my sins to you and stopped trying to hide my guilt. I said to myself, "I will confess my rebellion to the LORD." And you forgave me!
All my guilt is gone.
PSALM 32:4–5 NLT

• • • • • • • • • • • • • • • • • •

A new school year began, and I found myself hanging out with a new crowd of people. They weren't Christians, and I started making small compromises—suddenly doing and saying things I would never normally say and do. I knew it was wrong; I felt guilt immediately. But I shoved it down and kept changing my behavior to fit in with these new friends.

But guilt and conviction never go away. No matter how much you try to ignore it, you still feel it. It weighs on you. It chips away at your joy and happiness until all you feel is the strain. I was so miserable I finally confessed my rebellion to God. A weight finally lifted off my spirit, and I felt free!

It wasn't easy facing the rejection of my new friends once I stopped mimicking their lifestyle, but it was worth it. I was free from guilt, and the joy and peace of being right with God far outweighed the temporary, destructive friendships I'd made.

Thank You, Lord, for convicting me and not leaving me alone until I'm right with You. Amen.

The king will answer, "Whenever you did it for any
of my people, no matter how unimportant
they seemed, you did it for me."
MATTHEW 25:40 CEV

• • • • • • • • • • • • • • • • • •

We all prefer to stay in our comfort zone and relate
with those who are like us or who we want to be like.
But Jesus tells us that when we love others who are in
need, we're serving and giving directly to Jesus. Who
do you pass every day in the halls at school or in your
neighborhood that could use some love and help? How
can you reach out to them? Could you befriend the
friendless? Buy supplies for someone who needs them?
Do you own clothes you don't wear that you could
donate?

Whether you hang with a tight group of friends
or find yourself wishing you had more, today's verse
applies to you. Don't be so cozy in your friendships that
you overlook or exclude others who desperately need
a friend. If you're looking for more friends, reach out in
friendship to someone you may normally ignore. There's
no better way to love Jesus than by loving the loveless or
those easily overlooked.

God, open my eyes to the people around me
who need Your love today. Show me how I can serve
You by serving the overlooked and "unimportant"
people I see every day. Amen.

Confess your sins to each other and pray for each other so God can heal you. When a believing person prays, great things happen.
JAMES 5:16 NCV

. . . .

I had a shameful secret. I was seriously attracted to our new youth leader. Fresh out of college and recently married, he was a charismatic guy and really good-looking. He never acted inappropriately toward me, but he made me tongue-tied and nervous. I did *not* want to have a crush on him. But I couldn't stop my feelings.

When the opportunity came to go on a three-week mission trip to Thailand, I felt God nudging me to go, but I hesitated to commit to the team. I didn't think I could be that close to our youth leader for that length of time. Finally, I confessed to a trusted friend about my attraction. And an amazing thing happened—as soon as I finally admitted it to someone and she prayed with me, the power it held over me was gone. I could interact with him in a normal way, freeing me to join the mission trip with a clear conscience.

Satan keeps us trapped when we hide our sins and shameful desires in the dark. Confession brings them into the light so God can bring healing and freedom. What dark secrets are you hiding? Who can you safely confess them to?

God, please give me courage to bring my struggles into the light and experience Your healing and freedom. Amen.

*Kind words are like honey—they cheer you up
and make you feel strong.*
PROVERBS 16:24 CEV

• • • • • • • • • • • • • • • • • •

It's not hard to say hurtful things—especially behind someone's back or by posting something online or in a text. It's even easier to be mean and hurtful when someone has been a jerk to you. Why be nice when they started it? But what comes out of your mouth shows what's inside your heart. If hurtful and hateful speech pours out, what does that say about the condition of your heart?

Kind words spread like honey—nourishing the malnourished and refreshing the soul. When kindness from your heart genuinely comes out in kind words *to* others and *about* others, not only will your words refresh people's hungry souls, but you'll feel better, too, for not playing dirty with anger and gossip. Honey is sweet to the taste and healthy for the body. Likewise, kind words benefit others as well as those who use them.

Whose actions tempt you to speak hurtful words—a sibling, parent, friend? How can you speak encouragement to them? What words would show them kindness?

*Lord, when I'm angry, please help me to calm myself
down before saying mean or hurtful things. Help me not
to get involved with gossip. Please change my heart and
make it pure so I can genuinely love and speak
kind words to others. Amen.*

*Thereafter, Hagar used another name to refer
to the LORD, who had spoken to her. She said,
"You are the God who sees me."*
GENESIS 16:13 NLT

• • • • • • • • • • • • • • • •

Hagar was a nobody, a servant in Abraham's household.
With no choice in the matter, she was forced to marry
Abraham so she could bear his children because Sarah,
his first wife, was barren. But when Hagar got pregnant,
Sarah grew jealous. She mistreated Hagar until Hagar
decided to run away. Pregnant, alone, and penniless,
Hagar probably felt utterly forgotten. No one saw her
plight. No one cared.

But God cared. He revealed Himself to her beside a
spring in the wilderness and gave her a promise and a
blessing. Stunned, Hagar thereafter referred to God as El-
roi, "God who sees me."

It's easy to roam the halls at school feeling unnoticed
and lonely. Even surrounded by a group of friends, you
can feel like no one really *knows* you, no one really *sees*
you. But God does. He knows your hurts, your fears, your
dreams, and your mistreatment. When you feel utterly
alone and invisible, pray to El-roi, the God who sees you.
And feel His loving presence and peace.

*Dear El-roi, thank You that I'm not invisible to You.
That You see the deepest parts of me and love me
and want to be with me. Please reveal Yourself to me
and help me know that I'm not alone. Amen.*

*Pile your troubles on G*OD*'s shoulders—he'll carry your load, he'll help you out.*
P*SALM* 55:22 MSG

. . . .

How much is too much? How busy is too busy? The answer is different for each person, but knowing your limits is helpful. You can borrow trouble by staying too busy or trying to take on too much.

The worst thing you can do is refuse God's help. He'll take as much stress and anxiety as you're willing to give. He'll never turn you away saying, "I'm taking a break from carrying your burdens. I'm really tired of the trouble you cause. Try again later." God is patient. His love means He's fully dependable. He said He'll carry your load, and He will.

We do a couple really foolish things. First we try to carry our own load, thinking we're strong enough. Second we try to manage the trouble on our own because we don't want to bother God. It's sort of like having a truck available to haul a load of bricks, but carrying them on your own because you don't want to turn the ignition switch. Trucks are intended to carry bricks. God intends to carry our burdens. The decision is easy. Give up the burdens.

Dear God, You want me to give up the stress that puts me in a bad place. Help me say no when necessary and allow You to carry the weight of all those things I can't handle or control. Amen.

"But I say, love your enemies! Pray for those who persecute you! In that way, you will be acting as true children of your Father in heaven."
MATTHEW 5:44–45 NLT

• • • • • • • • • • • • • • • • • • • •

We all have people we don't like—and people we *really* don't like. You might even call them your enemies. Whether it's a long-time rival, a bully at school, or someone who always mistreats you, it's easy to return hate with hate.

It was accepted in Jesus' time, much like ours, to love friends and hate enemies. But Jesus takes what's accepted and puts a radical twist on it by saying we should not only love our friends, but also our enemies. And just as we pray for our friends, we should pray for our enemies. Not spiteful prayers demanding justice and vindication, but loving and kind prayers for the people who mistreat us.

If we hate our enemies, we're just like everyone else. And we're not supposed to be like everyone else! God wants us to be distinct from the world, pointing others to Jesus by what we believe, think, say, and do.

So what enemy can you pray for today?

Jesus, it's not easy returning kindness for hatred and prayers for pain. But You know that. You were treated horribly during Your ministry, and You loved and forgave. Help me to have Your spirit and strength to do the same. Amen.

*Go ahead and be angry. You do well to be angry—but
don't use your anger as fuel for revenge. And don't stay
angry. Don't go to bed angry. Don't give the Devil
that kind of foothold in your life.*
 EPHESIANS 4:26–27 MSG

. . . .

A friend made a comment that really upset me. Instead
of saying something at the time, I stayed silent. But my
mind wouldn't let it go. I mulled on it all evening, got a
restless night's sleep, and still woke up bothered by it. As
much as I tried to push it aside, the more I dwelled on it,
the angrier I became.

So I finally addressed the issue with her. We talked it
through, she apologized, and I could finally let the matter
go. Whew! I felt so much better!

When things bother you, God's Word says it's okay
to be angry. But how you handle your anger—that's what
makes the difference. It's not okay to hold it in and let
your anger start affecting your treatment of someone—
giving the cold shoulder, being rude, or making sharp
comments. Address the issue, clear the air, and let it go.

What grudges are you holding on to—against
your parents, siblings, or friends? How can you start
conversations to address the conflict and express your
hurt?

*God, help me have the courage to talk about things that
bother me instead of letting it fester inside. Amen.*

"If you love me, you will obey my commands."
JOHN 14:15 NCV

. . . .

A lot of people say they love God. But not everyone who says they love God obeys Him and does what He says. Can you love God and be disobedient? No.

Your obedience to God *proves* your love for Him. If you love God, you will listen to Him. If you don't love God, you will disobey Him and do whatever you want. You can't both love and rebel against God at the same time. This is why Jesus said, "Why do you call me, 'Lord, Lord,' but do not do what I say?" (see Luke 6:46).

We naturally want to please those we love. It hurts us when we know we've hurt or disappointed someone we care about. So we strive to show our love in ways that please the other person. We may not *like* doing the dishes, but we know it really blesses Mom. We may dislike basketball, but we attend a game anyway because our friend enjoys it. Similarly, our obedience to God shows Him how much we love Him and want to please Him.

Actions win over words every time. How well are you loving God?

Lord, please forgive me for disobeying You at times.
I truly want to follow You and make You Lord of my life.
Help me live in obedience so my love for You shows
and my life is pleasing to You. Amen.

*Obviously, I'm not trying to win the approval of people,
but of God. If pleasing people were my goal,
I would not be Christ's servant.*
GALATIANS 1:10 NLT

• • • • • • • • • • • • • • • • • • • •

Paul confronted the believers in Galatia for following
a twisted version of the Gospel that wasn't the true
message at all (see v. 6). Paul stated there is only one
true message—the way of Jesus—but people were
confusing His message, changing it, and causing people
to turn away from the real truth (see v. 7). So Paul
strongly called for punishment of those who changed
God's message (see vv. 8–9).

Paul clearly stepped on some toes! He knew his
words would offend some people, but he didn't care (see
v. 10). He wasn't out to win people's approval—he only
wanted to please God.

What truths in God's Word are hard for you to
swallow? Do you find yourself trying to be "tolerant" and
watering down God's message so it's more comfortable
for you and others in our culture? Are you afraid to
offend others by sharing God's truth?

Who are you trying to please? Others or Him?

*God, help me boldly share the truth in love.
Help me to be sensitive to others, but not back
down from what I know is true from Your Word.
I just want to please You. Amen.*

Nothing to Be Embarrassed About

Always be prepared to give an answer to everyone who asks you to give the reason for the hope that you have. But do this with gentleness and respect.
1 PETER 3:15 NIV

* * * * * * * * * * * * * * * * * *

Peter was a disciple of Jesus. He was impulsive. He acted before he thought. It got him into trouble.

One of his "awkward" moments came a few hours before Jesus' death. Peter was in the crowd hoping to see Jesus. Three times he was asked if he was a follower of Jesus. He said no. The man who wrote, "Always be prepared to give an answer to everyone who asks you to give the reason for the hope that you have," didn't give a truthful answer that night.

Jesus forgave Peter. He told Peter that he would be used to start the church. The lessons Peter learned helped him understand the hope we have is worth sharing and there is no reason to be embarrassed. People want to know what makes us different. We should quit hiding the many gifts God has asked us to distribute. The greatest of these gifts is love.

Dear God, You don't want me to respond like Peter, but I'm pretty sure I have. When others ask if I know You, it's easy to say no. I do follow You, and You're worth sharing. Amen.

Faith

To have faith is to be sure of the things we hope for,
to be certain of the things we cannot see.
HEBREWS 11:1 GNT

• •

"God, I don't get it! Why did _____ happen? I just don't understand!"

Ever had these thoughts? Everyone does. These thoughts can be accompanied with anger, grief, disappointment, or even a sense of rebellion—wanting to turn your back on God. But circumstances that prompt these thoughts are what test and prove your trust in God. *Faith* is to believe in God's goodness, love, and sovereign control. . .no matter what. It's being *certain* of God's good character, even when you may not see it. It's being *sure* that God loves you and is taking care of you, even when He feels distant and silent and like He's not even there. Faith says, "Even when I don't understand, I will choose You, God. I will trust You, no matter what."

Does God have your full faith? Can you trust Him, whatever happens?

Sovereign God, sometimes I just don't understand
why things happen. I want to trust that You do have
good plans and something positive can come out
of all this bad. Despite my circumstances,
I choose to trust You. Amen.

Then I saw "a new heaven and a new earth," for the first heaven and the first earth had passed away. . . And I heard a loud voice from the throne saying, "Look! God's dwelling place is now among the people, and he will dwell with them. . . . 'He will wipe every tear from their eyes. There will be no more death' or mourning or crying or pain, for the old order of things has passed away."
REVELATION 21:1, 3–4 NIV

• • • • • • • • • • • • • • • • • •

At the core of the Christian faith is the belief that we'll spend eternity with God if we confess our sins and put our faith in Him. But how often do we really think about the hope of heaven? Or imagine it? Or study what the Bible says about it? Most of the time heaven is this vague hope that we'll join God "somewhere up there" when we die.

But eternity with God is an exciting thing! Revelation 21 says God will live among us—we'll actually *see* Him (see v. 3)! There will be no sun or moon because God's glory will be bright enough to provide all light (see v. 23). God's light will eternally shine, and there will never be night (see v. 25). There will be no pain, no death, no shame or deceit (see vv. 4, 27), only happiness, joy, and perfection.

Imagine!

Lord, the hope of heaven overwhelms me. Thank You for saving me! I can't wait to live with You. Amen.

*Think about what is up there,
not about what is here on earth.*
COLOSSIANS 3:2 CEV

• • • • • • • • • • • • • • • • •

I love getting outside and taking walks or hiking trails.
But too often my gaze stays on my feet and the path
immediately before me. I consciously have to pull my
eyes up and remind myself to take in the beauty of my
surroundings as I walk.

Life is like that, too. It's so easy to keep our eyes
focused on the immediate—schoolwork, athletic
performance, feeling accepted, frustration with parents,
etc. It's hard to look past tomorrow, let alone beyond
high school! But God wants you to pull your eyes all
the way up—to Him. He wants you to look beyond your
present circumstances and remember what's truly
important—eternal life with Him.

So release your worries, realign your priorities, and
let go of the temporary things here on earth. Keep your
eyes and your mind focused on what truly lasts. Look
up and see the beauty of God all around you instead of
staying focused on the dull path before you.

*Thank You, Father, for the hope of heaven. Help me to lift
my eyes and thoughts above my present circumstances
to You and be filled with joy, peace, and hope. Amen.*

Charm can be deceiving, and beauty fades away, but a woman who honors the Lord deserves to be praised.
PROVERBS 31:30 CEV

• • • • • • • • • • • • • • • • • • •

What does our culture value in women? Beauty and charm. You can't escape it. Just look at the magazine headlines in the checkout aisle. "25 Ways to Lose Weight Before Summer!" "15 Ways to Charm Your Man." "10 Ways to Look Sexy." "5 Ways to Catch His Interest." In school, who's obsessed with looking beautiful and being liked? Um, pretty much everyone!

God tells us plainly that charm is misleading and beauty doesn't last. He puts value in what's truly important and never fades—our relationship with Him.

Where are you placing your value? In your looks? Your charming personality? Your academic smarts? Your athletic ability? Or do you find your value and worth in God?

A girl who is confident in herself because she is confident in the Lord, who seeks God's approval above all others, who models God's behavior and actions—*that's* a girl worth admiring!

God, I know it's not wrong to want to feel pretty and liked, but I shouldn't let those things define me. I am Your child and Your creation—and that makes me valued and beautiful! Amen.

"If we are thrown into the blazing furnace, the God we serve is able to deliver us from it, and he will deliver us from Your Majesty's hand. But even if he does not, we want you to know, Your Majesty, that we will not serve your gods or worship the image of gold you have set up."
DANIEL 3:17–18 NIV

• • • • • • • • • • • • • • • • • • •

Sometimes being a Christian has consequences. People might make fun of you, bully you, or label you as *weird*. Sometimes you won't be able to do what your friends are doing. And in many cases, especially in other countries, being a Christian can mean facing physical harm.

God can save us and protect us from these consequences. But what if He doesn't? Shadrach, Meshach, and Abednego understood that God was powerful enough to save them from any persecution they might face. But they also understood that God doesn't always "deliver" us in the way we expect and allows us to face consequences and experience pain.

Is your faith as strong as Shadrach's, Meshach's, and Abednego's? Are you resolved to obey God, even if He doesn't keep the pain away? Are you committed to follow Him—no matter what?

Jesus, help me not to give in when I feel pressure to go against You. Help me stand strong in my faith and have the courage to face whatever happens. Amen.

*Yet I am always with you; you hold me by my
right hand. You guide me with your counsel,
and afterward you will take me into glory.*
PSALM 73:23–24 NIV

• • • • • • • • • • • • • • • • • •

Sometimes life just doesn't seem fair. Right?
Nonbelievers seem to have better lives and fewer
worries. The jerks get favored while the good guys are
overlooked. Cheaters get ahead while those who play by
the rules suffer. So. Not. Fair.

Asaph, the writer of Psalm 73, struggled with the
same complaint. He envied nonbelievers because their
life seemed blessed (see vv. 2–14). The unfairness greatly
distressed him until he realized their final destiny (see v.
17). They lived on slippery ground (see v. 18), and their
eventual judgment would be swift and hard (see vv.
19–20). Asaph realized that though life may not play out
fairly, it's far better to be close to God (see v. 28).

Being a Christian doesn't mean life will be easier
or perfectly just. We'll suffer. Things won't be fair.
Sometimes the bad guys will win. . .for now. But we have
God on our side and His presence in our life. He'll make
everything right in the end.

*God, injustice makes me so mad, but I am comforted
that You are always with Your people. You never leave us,
and we have eternal life with You. Thank You that
fairness will win in the end. Amen.*

"The joy of the LORD is your strength."
NEHEMIAH 8:10 NIV

· · · · · · · · · · · · · · · · · · ·

Sometimes life is just *drama*. People let you down and disappoint you. You suffer an unexpected loss. You battle the constant feeling of not quite liking who you are and wishing you were just a little different. Add stress, growing responsibilities, and pressure to perform, and life suddenly seems overwhelming and joyless. Emotions weigh like heavy rain clouds, ready to break at any moment.

It's easy to believe the sun is gone on cloudy, stormy days. But the truth is, the sun is always shining in the sky—even if thick thunderheads block your view. The same is true of God's joy. It's real, it's there, and it never goes away, no matter how you feel or what you go through. When you have gray days, you only have to reach out to the joy of the Lord to find strength. Look beyond the clouds—beyond your situation—to soak in the rays of God's joy and find the strength you need to face the day.

Lord, my spirit just seems heavy. Shine Your joy into my life and give me the strength I need to make it through this time. Help me not to wallow in the clouds, but to look beyond my circumstances for the joy You provide. Amen.

Who's Your Umpire?

*And let the peace (soul harmony which comes)
from Christ rule (act as umpire continually) in your hearts
[deciding and settling with finality all questions that arise
in your minds, in that peaceful state] to which
as [members of Christ's] one body you
were also called [to live].*
COLOSSIANS 3:15 AMP

. . . .

When you have a decision to make, everyone always says to "pray about it." But what does that mean? Okay, so I ask God about what He wants me to do. . .then what?

Then you wait for peace.

God's Word says to let peace be our umpire. When an opportunity or decision is pitched your way, God stands behind you as the umpire. He'll tell you whether or not to swing for the ball by the peace you feel. What decision makes you feel one-hundred-percent at peace—no doubts, no nagging questions, no second-guessing? Just a calm sense of rightness. That's how you know what God wants you to do.

Any decision that doesn't bring peace means it's out! God wants you to turn it down or pass it by because something better is coming your way or maybe now isn't the right time.

What decisions are you facing today? What is your sense of peace telling you to do?

*God, thank You for letting peace be my umpire,
guiding me about what to do. Help me to strongly
sense Your peace as I make decisions. Amen.*

"Simply put, if you're not willing to take what is dearest to you, whether plans or people, and kiss it good-bye, you can't be my disciple."
LUKE 14:33 MSG

• • • • • • • • • • • •

Following God isn't just about following rules, going to church, and reading your Bible. It's not about being good and waiting for God's approval in return. Or making your own plans and asking for His blessing on what *you* decide. Following God means total surrender.

Jesus demands *everything* from you—your rights, your dreams, your plans for the future, your life.

Now, wait a second! That's so harsh! The cost *is* high, but the reward is even greater. Following Jesus wasn't meant to be easy. It demands sacrifice, and it shows what you truly love. If you love someone or something more than you love God, you won't be willing to give it up. And God wants to be first in your life, your greatest love.

Are you willing to follow Him? What do you need to surrender?

Whew, Jesus. You ask a lot from me. But I also know that You gave up everything for me—leaving Your home in heaven, restricting Yourself in a human body, and dying a horrible death to pay for my sins. I want to love You that much, too. Lord, I surrender to You. Amen.

Leap of Faith

Then Peter got down out of the boat, walked on the water and came toward Jesus. But when he saw the wind, he was afraid and, beginning to sink, cried out, "Lord, save me!" Immediately Jesus reached out his hand and caught him. "You of little faith," he said, "why did you doubt?"
MATTHEW 14:29–31 NIV

• • • • • • • • • • • • • • • • • •

It's one thing to *say* we trust God. But when we actually have to do it—it can be pretty scary! To step out of a boat onto solid ground, no problem! To step out of a boat into the middle of a lake to *walk* on water during a windy night with no life vest? Um, seriously?

Even for Peter, that was a scary leap! But the moment Peter cried out, Jesus was right there, catching him, keeping him tight in His grip. Yes, trusting God can be scary. But He's always right there to catch us, never leaving us, never letting go.

Taking a leap of faith means stepping out of the familiar into something that may seem crazy, but experiencing the joy and warmth of the Father's arms when He catches you. It means feeling the intensity of His grip on you. And suddenly, His voice, His touch, and His presence become tangible in your life.

God, trusting You can be difficult. Help me to trust You and experience You like Peter did. Help me to feel Your grip on my life. Amen.

If we are unfaithful, he remains faithful,
for he cannot deny who he is.
2 TIMOTHY 2:13 NLT

• • • • • • • • • • • • • • •

Commitment doesn't mean much these days. Where can we learn about faithfulness when parents call it quits and give up on each other, or a boyfriend says he loves you then ditches you for another girl, or your best friend does something that betrays you? Where is the model of faithfulness when almost every movie or story tells you it's okay to date around and experiment—and something's wrong with you if you don't?

We're all guilty of breaking promises and hurting others who trusted us. And we're also guilty of not remaining faithful to God. We all make mistakes. We all eventually do things we know we shouldn't. But that's the beauty of God's grace! In our faithlessness, God remains faithful. He's our northern star, our guiding light, our steady rock that never changes. He is who He says He is—and He can't deny His very nature. God is our perfect model of faithfulness.

He'll never turn His back on you, never leave you, never break your trust. No matter what!

Lord, it's so reassuring that no matter how much I fail,
no matter how much I turn my back on You, no matter
how bad I mess up, You'll never give up on me.
Thank You, Father, for Your faithfulness! Amen.

This is the confidence we have in approaching God:
that if we ask anything according to his will, he hears us.
And if we know that he hears us—whatever we ask—
we know that we have what we asked of him.
1 JOHN 5:14–15 NIV

• • • • • • • • • • • • • • • •

All good things come to those who wait. Right? But sometimes we wait and wait and nothing happens. We pray, and God doesn't answer.

Many times there's growth that needs to take place in our life before we're ready for God's reply. Sometimes we hear from God only after we've persisted in asking (see Luke 18:1–8). Persistently praying also reveals our faithfulness and teaches us to keep praying without giving up (see Galatians 6:9).

Sometimes God's answer is simply no. Are you still able to trust God and believe He is good when He doesn't allow you to have what you want? Is He enough? Or are you clinging too hard to something else?

God could be denying your prayers because you're asking with wrong motives (see James 4:3). If your request comes from selfishness to satisfy yourself and not to glorify God, chances are God isn't going to grant it.

When you pray, know that God has a plan. He is good, and He will not withhold any good thing from you!

Lord, teach me to pray according to Your will, with pure motives and with patient persistence. Amen.

A Very Bad Day

"I came naked from my mother's womb, and I will be naked when I leave. The LORD gave me what I had, and the LORD has taken it away. Praise the name of the LORD!"
JOB 1:21 NLT

• • • • • • • • • • • • • • • • • • •

Job was a very rich man. But he lost *everything*—all his livestock, farmhands, servants, and children—in *one day* (see vv. 13–18)! In a flash, he went from wealthy to bankrupt, from proud papa to childless man. Just. Like. That. But he didn't respond with anger and shouting. Undone, he fell to the ground *in worship* (see v. 20)! With tears streaming down his face, he praised the Lord.

When we suffer, it's natural to question God—to ask why and seek understanding. As Job continued to suffer, he sure asked tough questions and demanded some answers from God. But God never explained Himself—He just said, "I'm big. I'm good. I'm in control. Will you trust Me?"

Do you trust God that much? When bad things happen or life takes a crazy curve, do you get angry or praise God amid the confusion and pain? Do you demand answers or simply trust God, even if you don't understand? Do you wrestle—or do you surrender?

God, sometimes it's hard to praise You, even when it hurts. To believe in Your goodness, even when nothing seems good. Help me to trust You and praise You like Job. Amen.

Get rid of all bitterness, rage and anger....Be kind and compassionate to one another, forgiving each other, just as in Christ God forgave you.
EPHESIANS 4:31–32 NIV

. . . .

Today's technology makes gossip a whole lot easier. It's so simple and easy to say things online about someone that you would never say face-to-face. Facebook, e-mail, blogs, texting, and IMs make it easy to engage in word wars that are less than encouraging and kind. And far more hurtful.

Watch what you say—especially in print. Don't engage in mean-spirited talk about others. If things are being said about you, don't respond angrily. Give yourself time to calm down and think of a gentle response. And always work to take the conversation offline and speak face-to-face or on the phone.

If verbal bullying continues in person or online, tell a trusted adult what's happening. If you know of someone being harassed, don't be a bystander! Gently shut down the conversation or stick up for the person. And if mean comments are flying around about you, work to forgive the person and respond with love and grace.

Lord, please forgive me for saying mean things about others, especially online. Help me to be kind and loving instead. Help me to forgive those who say mean things about me and to respond the way You want me to, not in hurt or anger. Amen.

Praise the LORD! Give thanks to the LORD,
for he is good! His faithful love endures forever.
PSALM 106:1 NLT

• • • • • • • • • • • • • • • • •

The Bible commands us to *praise* the Lord and *give thanks* to Him because His faithful love endures forever. Why should God's people be commanded to do something that should come naturally?

How many people have you told about that amazing movie you saw? The gripping book you read? The fun song you heard? Did you speak highly of it and express enthusiastic approval toward it? If so, you praised the thing you enjoyed.

If you're not praising God, examine why. Have you stopped enjoying God? Why? It's easy to lose sight of who God is and what He's done. God can become like an old Christmas gift—we experience joy and excitement upon first receiving Him, but after a while He gets shoved in a closet and forgotten about. But God's love is faithful and will always be there for you, even when your love for Him fades. The love of God never expires—He loves you now and for eternity. No matter what.

Thank You, God!

Lord, I praise You today for Your incredible love.
Even when I neglect You, ignore You, or avoid You,
You still faithfully love me. Your love is powerful,
God, and worthy of my praise! Amen.

Her sister, Mary, sat at the Lord's feet, listening to what he taught. But Martha was distracted by the big dinner she was preparing.
LUKE 10:39–40 NLT

. . . .

Read your Bible? Check! Prayed? Check! Went to youth group? Check! Signed up for a mission trip? Check!

It's pretty easy to busy ourselves serving God and to view Christianity as a list of tasks to complete. Don't get me wrong. . .reading your Bible, praying, and going to youth group are great things! But there's more to it than that. Jesus also wants us to sit, be still, listen, grow, and worship Him. This doesn't mean spending time with Him so we can check it off our task list for the day; it's coming to Him and being still and sitting with Him for however long it takes.

Mary knew what was important—sitting and being with Jesus. Martha became so distracted with serving Jesus that she forgot to just sit and be with Him. How about you? Are you so easily distracted by completing tasks and serving God that you forget to just stop and be? Your value isn't in what you accomplish, give, or do. Your value is in who you are—a daughter of the King!

Lord, forgive me for sometimes treating my time with You as a task to accomplish. Life can get so busy that spending time with You is just one more thing to do. Help me slow down and just be. Amen.

Everything they do is just to show off in front of others. . . .
They love the best seats at banquets and the front seats
in the meeting places. And when they are in the market,
they like to have people greet them as their teachers.
MATTHEW 23:5–7 CEV

• • • • • • • • • • • • • • • •

The Pharisees were all about status. They flaunted their
position as religious leaders, strutting around in pride
and arrogance. And Jesus condemned them for it.

It's easy to point our fingers at the Pharisees and say
how bad they were. But we are status-seekers, too. Are
you tempted to hide your friendship with someone when
the more popular kids come around? Do you always try
to sit where you know you'll be noticed? Do you drive
yourself in academics or athletics because you seek the
attention that comes with it? Do you wear name-brand
clothes because you want the status of being cool and
stylish?

Jesus says, "If you put yourself above others, you
will be put down. But if you humble yourself, you will be
honored" (Matthew 23:12 CEV). Status among our peers
isn't what's truly important. Make it a point to serve
instead of show off.

God, please forgive me for thinking I'm better than
others and for seeking the status and approval of my
friends instead of You. Help me to serve others,
like You, by focusing on others and not myself. Amen.

"I've had it with you! You're hopeless, you religion scholars, you Pharisees! Frauds! Your lives are roadblocks to God's kingdom."
MATTHEW 23:13 MSG

. . . .

"Christians are just a bunch of hypocrites!"

We've all heard someone say it. Hypocrisy is one of the biggest reasons nonbelievers want nothing to do with Christianity. Pastors are caught stealing church funds. Christian girls get pregnant. Christian guys are pulled over and slapped with a DUI. Sin has pretty big consequences.

As a Christian, you represent Jesus to everyone around you. You aren't perfect, and you won't represent Him perfectly all the time. But you need to remove the roadblocks to God's kingdom by matching your actions with your words. Do people see you going to church on Sunday but cussing and cutting down others during the week? Do they see you pray before your meals but be disrespectful to your parents and teachers? Do they know you're a Christian but are turned off by your arrogance and pride?

The world is watching, whether you're aware or not. Are your words and actions inviting people into heaven—or turning them away?

Lord, I know I mess up and seem like a hypocrite. I'm glad people can look to You as the perfect example instead of me. But I don't want to turn people away from You because of the sin in my life. Show me how I need to change so others are drawn to You through me. Amen.

"You Pharisees are so careful to clean the outside of the cup and the dish, but inside you are filthy—full of greed and wickedness! Fools! Didn't God make the inside as well as the outside? So clean the inside by giving gifts to the poor, and you will be clean all over."
LUKE 11:39–41 NLT

. . . .

Jesus was ticked off at the Pharisees because they had impure motives. They did all the right things—but for all the wrong reasons. They were so careful to follow the rules and be "good," but their hearts were self-righteous and full of pride. Jesus saw through their sham and said when their motives were pure, then their "good works" would be acceptable.

Jesus isn't concerned about our behavior—He's concerned about our hearts. Because when your heart is right, then proper behavior will naturally follow. Why do you attend church? Because your parents make you or because you want to? Why do you read your Bible? Because you want to or because you feel guilty if you don't?

Jesus isn't concerned about you following a set of rules—doing what you're *supposed* to do. He wants you to follow Him willingly, because you *want* to. Ask yourself: Why do I do what I do? Whom am I doing it for?

Jesus, forgive me for doing things because they'll make me look good on the outside, when I have the wrong motive on the inside. Clean me from the inside out. Amen.

When doubts filled my mind, your comfort gave me renewed hope and cheer.
PSALM 94:19 NLT

. . . .

Sometimes the pain we feel emotionally seems more hurtful than pain we feel physically. You can stick some ointment and a bandage on a cut or take medicine for a pounding headache—but how do you heal a worried mind and an anxious heart? Many times we try different ways to cope with the pain or make it go away, but that's not the answer. It might numb the pain, but it doesn't heal it.

We're not equipped to fix large hurts by ourselves. We need God's touch in our lives. When you're really hurting, do you give God room to soothe the pain? Do you share your hurt with Him and let His Word comfort you? Or do you feel shame in approaching Him because the root of the pain is your disobedience to Him? Whatever you're facing, don't block God out. Share your struggle with a spiritual big sister, and open yourself to allow God's soothing touch in your life, wiping away the worries and burdens and giving you joy.

God, I don't like feeling or facing pain. When it comes, help me come to You for comfort. Calm my anxious heart. Help me feel Your touch in my life like healing ointment to my soul. Amen.

Everyone must submit to governing authorities. For all authority comes from God, and those in positions of authority have been placed there by God.
ROMANS 13:1 NLT

· · · · · · · · · · · · · · · · · · ·

Politics. . .blech! Who cares what's going on in the government? It's hard to understand what the news anchors are talking about, and it's *bo*-ring anyway. God's got it all covered, right?

While the Bible is full of stories of God moving people and nations into power and out of power, that doesn't mean we stick our head in the sand and ignore what's happening politically. We have an amazing blessing in America to vote and shape our government. Our active participation or passive disinterest will directly affect our future.

You will be a voting citizen someday. It's important that you pay attention in history class, discuss with your teachers and parents the problems and decisions our nation faces, and learn to think critically about the decisions political leaders make.

Most importantly, we need to pray for our leaders—locally, statewide, and nationally. Pray for God to place the correct people in office, for corruption to be exposed, and for cooperation among political parties so they can work together for the common good.

Lord, I pray for our government. The problems are many, but I pray that You would lead and guide our leaders to make the best decisions for our country. Amen.

Who's the Bomb?

Don't think you are better than you really are.
Be honest in your evaluation of yourselves,
measuring yourselves by the faith God has given us.
ROMANS 12:3 NLT

• • • • • • • • • • • • • • • • • • •

It's *so* tempting to bask in others' praise, isn't it? To glory in your athletic ability and strut down the halls at school. To pat yourself on the back for your academic achievements. To take credit for your musical ability or physical appearance. To pride yourself in the fact that at least you aren't like *them*.

But the credit doesn't belong to you. God made you and gave you the talents you have. We owe everything to Him. And without His grace, we wouldn't be anybody. So put arrogance aside and thank God for blessing you. When others praise you, use the opportunity to point them to Jesus, the giver of all good gifts. Use your talents for God's glory, not your own.

Please forgive me, Jesus. Help me to use my talents for Your kingdom, to use them as a witness to others, and not for my own personal gain or fame. Amen.

Everything that is hidden will be found out, and every secret will be known. Whatever you say in the dark will be heard when it is day. Whatever you whisper in a closed room will be shouted from the housetops.
LUKE 12:2–3 CEV

• • • • • • • • • • • • • • • • • •

Have you ever breathed a sigh of relief when your sibling took the blame for something you did? Feel lucky that you didn't get caught cheating on your history quiz? Ever watch something you knew you shouldn't? You may think you got away with it, but God sees everything. One day everything will be revealed, and everyone will be judged.

Don't be caught like the Pharisees! Jesus revealed them to the world for who they really were. The Pharisees weren't upstanding religious leaders to be imitated and followed; they were greedy, self-righteous, wicked men whom Jesus publicly judged and condemned.

Keeping up a good image and hiding their sin—that was the Pharisees' main goal. Scrap what others think and make pleasing Jesus your main goal. It doesn't matter if you will or won't get away with something here on earth. You won't get away with it with God.

*God, help me to come clean about my sin
and not hide it or let others take the blame for it.
Help me be more concerned about pleasing You
than maintaining a good image. Amen.*

Noah was a righteous man, blameless among the people of his time, and he walked faithfully with God.
GENESIS 6:9 NIV

. . . .

Is it more important to be noticed by others or by God? God, of course! But why do we usually place more importance on being noticed by others? We care what guys think about us; we like it when we catch their eye. We want to be noticed by girls as someone cool and fun to include. We find value in being noticed. It makes us feel important, liked, and special.

How do you think the people of Noah's time viewed him? Would they have noticed the things he did and wanted to be his BFF? Would they want to take selfies with Noah and post them on Instagram? Probably not. Most likely, Noah was always the odd one out and ridiculed.

But that didn't matter to Noah because he was more concerned about pleasing God rather than others. When you walk faithfully with God, the right type of people will notice you. And those are the friends you want.

How do you try to be noticed? What are your motives? Are you placing more value on others' acceptance and approval rather than God's?

God, please help me to be like Noah and walk faithfully with You, no matter how others treat me. Help me not to change my behavior or compromise my values just to be noticed and liked. Amen.

*"Make yourselves holy for I am holy. . . . I am GOD
who brought you up out of the land of
Egypt. Be holy because I am holy."*
LEVITICUS 11:44–45 MSG

. . . .

God wants us to be happy, right? Well, yes. But God is far
more concerned with our holiness than our happiness.
Numerous times throughout the Bible, God commands
His people to be holy. Not once does He command us to
be happy.

While God does desire to bless us, He has a far
greater purpose for us than happiness. When we choose
to follow God, we leave our old habits behind and
become a new person. We strive to become holy as God
is holy—reflecting His goodness and character to all
those around us. Be careful not to make decisions based
on how happy it will make you. "It's okay to do this, have
this, or be with this person because God wants me to be
happy" is dangerous logic. Instead ask yourself, "Is doing
this, having this, or being with this person going to draw
me closer to God and help me grow spiritually?"

Paul tells Timothy, "For God saved us and called us
to live a holy life" (2 Timothy 1:9 NLT). Are you pursuing
happiness more than holiness?

*God, help me to care more about holiness than
happiness. Give me strength to sacrifice happiness
when holiness requires it and trust that You
will bring joy and blessing from my obedience. Amen.*

God Is Watching

The eyes of the Lord are everywhere,
keeping watch on the wicked and the good.
PROVERBS 15:3 NIV

• • • • • • • • • • • • • • • • • • •

My parents had rules. And one of those rules restricted me from watching any movie above a PG rating without their prior permission. There were countless times I'd spend the night at a friend's house, and she'd pop in a PG-13 movie.

It's just PG-13, I'd think to myself. *My parents won't need to know. I don't need to say anything.*

But God's conviction and my conscience would never let me get away with it. I knew God was watching, even if my parents weren't. And God wanted me to obey my parents. So I'd call and ask for permission before any movies started—every time.

A lot of times I felt like an idiot in front of my friends, especially if my parents didn't want me to watch the movie and I had to suggest something else. But the momentary embarrassment was worth the rewards. I didn't have to battle a guilty conscience. I built trust with my parents, which eventually gave me greater freedom from the rules. And most of all, I know I pleased God with my obedience to Him and my parents.

What areas of compromise tempt you the most?

God, help me to listen when You convict me and do
the right thing, even if it means I'll look foolish
or feel embarrassed. You are always watching,
and I want to please You. Amen.

Do everything without complaining or arguing, so that
you may be innocent and pure as God's perfect children,
who live in a world of corrupt and sinful people.
PHILIPPIANS 2:14–15 GNT

• • • • • • • • • • • • • • • •

"It's not fair! I never get to do what I want. I don't have any friends. And no one else's life is harder than mine!"

When life gets hard, sometimes we want to throw ourselves a big ol' pity party. Why do *I* have to clean the house? Why can't *I* spend the night at my friend's house? Why do *I* have to work so hard while everyone else has fun? Poor me! So we get an attitude and moan and complain and make sure everyone knows how sorry they should feel for us.

If anyone had the right to throw a pity party, it was Paul. He was whipped five times, beaten with rods three times, pelted with stones once, shipwrecked three times, imprisoned multiple times, and lived constantly in danger (see 2 Corinthians 11:24–26). And yet he never complained and joyfully offered his life as a sacrifice for others and for God (see Philippians 2:17–18).

Our selfishness shows when we drown ourselves in self-pity because everything becomes about *us* instead of *others*. How can you adjust your attitude today?

God, please help me not to focus on me and my
circumstances, but to have a servant's heart that is willing
to help others and work hard without complaining. Amen.

All athletes are disciplined in their training.
They do it to win a prize that will fade away,
but we do it for an eternal prize.
1 CORINTHIANS 9:25 NLT

• • • • • • • • • • • • • • • • • • • •

Sometimes it's hard to worship, because you just don't feel like it. You don't want to be at church. You don't want to pray. You don't want to read your Bible. You just want to leave God alone for a while and do what you want.

A relationship with God is just like any other commitment—it takes work. You may not feel like going to swim practice every day or doing your homework after school, but you do it anyway. Sure, maybe you're only doing it because you have to. But you're also doing it because on a deeper level, you want to—you want to improve your swim times and keep your grades up.

God is no different. We may not always *feel* like worshipping Him or spending time with Him, but we need to discipline ourselves to do it anyway. Only when we're disciplined and stay committed—not just showing up to practice here and there, but *every* day—will we see growth.

God, help me to discipline myself to work at my
relationship with You. A lot of times I don't feel like it,
but I know putting in the time and effort will help me
grow spiritually—and that's a lasting prize
worth pursuing. Amen.

Entitled

*You must have the same attitude that Christ Jesus had.
Though he was God, he did not think of equality with God
as something to cling to. Instead, he gave up his divine
privileges; he took the humble position of a slave and was
born as a human being. When he appeared in
human form, he humbled himself in obedience to
God and died a criminal's death on a cross.*
PHILIPPIANS 2:5–8 NLT

• • • • • • • • • • • • • • • • • •

Entitlement has become an epidemic in our country.
The belief that you have the right to have, do, or get
something, or that you *deserve* to be given something, is
a disease that cripples you and those around you.

Jesus never felt entitled. He was almighty, infinitely
powerful, and deserving of honor and glory, but He gave
up His divine rights and privileges and didn't cling to
them. He willingly lowered Himself and limited Himself
as a human being, even dying the most shameful death
possible.

What rights and privileges are you clinging to? What
do you complain about giving up?

*Jesus, please help me to have an attitude like You.
You willingly humbled Yourself and let go. When life
doesn't seem fair or demands a sacrifice, help me
do the same. Amen.*

Jesus said, "That is why I tell you not to worry about everyday life—whether you have enough food to eat or enough clothes to wear. For life is more than food, and your body more than clothing. . . . Can all your worries add a single moment to your life? . . . These things dominate the thoughts of unbelievers all over the world, but your Father already knows your needs. Seek the Kingdom of God above all else, and he will give you everything you need."
LUKE 12:22–23, 25, 30–31 NLT

• • • • • • • • • • • • • • • • • • •

I get it. Worries plague you from everywhere—whether you look fat, whether eating something will make you gain weight, how your hair looks, how your makeup looks, how trendy your clothes are (or aren't), whether or not girls like you, whether or not *boys* like you, how well you're doing in school, how well you're performing at practice. . .worry, worry, worry.

That's a big burden to carry! But Jesus says we don't have to carry it. If we seek God above all else, everything will fall into line. The weight of "success" and "performance" and "being good enough" doesn't fall on your shoulders. Everything—*everything*—is God's to work out, and all you're required to do is seek Him.

Dump those worries, girlfriend! Trade them for the freedom and peace Jesus wants to give.

Jesus, I give all my worries to You. Help me to seek You above all else. Amen.

Be Content

They are like hungry dogs that are never satisfied.
They are like shepherds who don't know what they
are doing. They all have gone their own way;
all they want to do is satisfy themselves.
ISAIAH 56:11 NCV

. . . .

By human nature, we want to satisfy ourselves. We want the latest technology, the newest phones, the trendy clothes. We want the best cable TV, the fastest Internet, the nicest cars. We want. . .we want. . .we want.

Even if we get what we want, it only satisfies for a while, and then we want something else. It's a cycle that doesn't end—a trap we must consciously avoid.

Instead of complaining about what you *don't* have, stop and be grateful for what you *do* have. When your friend shows off her new iPhone, instead of being jealous, be grateful you have a cell phone, even if it's "just a flip phone." When your parents steer you toward the sale racks or thrift stores instead of brand-new, full-price clothes, be thankful they're even able to provide you with new clothing.

The secret of contentment is being grateful for what you have instead of searching for something to satisfy you. How content are you?

Lord, my human nature sees something new
and shiny, and I can't help but want it. I see something
my friend has, and I can't help being jealous.
Change my attitude. Help me be content
and grateful for what I do have. Amen.

If you honor your father and mother, "things will go well
for you, and you will have a long life on the earth."
EPHESIANS 6:3 NLT

• • • • • • • • • • • • • • • • • •

Parents may be annoying at times, but they do *a lot* for
you. They work hard to provide money for you to buy
new clothes, join athletic teams, have a cell phone and
computer, and have food to eat. They run you around
to all your practices and activities. They pay for you to
attend summer camp or go on a family vacation.

Parents aren't perfect and everyone has faults, but
spend time today honoring your parents. Make a list of
everything they do and provide for you. How can you
make their burden easier? How can you help out around
the house? Maybe you can start doing your own laundry
instead of expecting your mom to do it, or you can put
the money you've earned toward summer camp fees
instead of blowing it at Starbucks or the movies. Why
not make dinner tonight for the family?

Whatever you decide to do, be sure to thank your
parents today for all they do for you.

God, I can't imagine life without my parents. I may not
always like them, but they take care of me the best they
can. If I had to survive on my own, I'd be in a really tough
place. So thank You for my mom and dad, and show me
how I can honor and thank them today. Amen.

You were saved by faith in God, who treats us much better than we deserve. This is God's gift to you, and not anything you have done on your own. It isn't something you have earned, so there is nothing you can brag about.
EPHESIANS 2:8-9 CEV

. . . .

God's love isn't something we have to earn. He gives it freely. But too often we fall into the trap of living a performance-based faith. If you don't attend youth group every week, you're not a good Christian. If you don't read your Bible or spend time with God every day, God isn't pleased with you. If you keep committing the same sin, no matter how hard you try, God looks at you with disappointment.

Lies. All of them.

God gives you grace. He doesn't want you to live up to some standard of performance, feeling like you need to do certain things to earn His acceptance. He loves you right now, as you are, no matter what.

So give yourself grace. Toss the guilt you've been living under and experience the true freedom the Lord gives. You're His daughter, and He loves you whether you have it all together or you're a total mess.

And that's the truth.

Thank You, God, that I don't need to live in guilt. I don't have to feel like I need to measure up to some standard to earn Your acceptance. Help me to live in that grace and freedom today. Amen.

Finally, be strong in the Lord and in his mighty power.
Put on the full armor of God, so that you can take
your stand against the devil's schemes.
EPHESIANS 6:10–11 NIV

• • • • • • • • • • • • • • • • • •

Before you head out the door each morning, you prepare yourself for the day. You get dressed, brush your teeth, style your hair, maybe apply some makeup, and hopefully grab some breakfast. Just as we prepare ourselves physically, we need to prepare ourselves spiritually. Putting on the armor of God isn't just about "praying it on." It's about living it—that's how we protect ourselves from the enemy's attacks.

Examine your armor:

•The belt of truth: Are you living in honesty and sincerity?

•The breastplate of righteousness: Are you living by faith, not works, and trusting Jesus' righteousness to cover you?

•Shoes of readiness that comes from the gospel of peace: Are you living in instant availability and mobility for God? Are you living in peace and ready to communicate the Gospel at a moment's notice?

•Shield of faith: Are you trusting God for protection and provision?

•Helmet of salvation: Are you living with hope and optimism in your thoughts and perspective?

•Sword of the Spirit: Are you memorizing and applying scripture?

Don't forget to get dressed spiritually!

Lord, help me be just as concerned about
how I look spiritually. Amen.

We gladly suffer, because we know that suffering helps us to endure. And endurance builds character, which gives us a hope that will never disappoint us.
ROMANS 5:3–5 CEV

• • • • • • • • • • • • • • • • • • •

No one *likes* to suffer, but suffering is necessary for growth. First, it teaches endurance. When there's no way out of a situation, you just have to slog through until it ends. And during the slogging, your character develops. You either whine and cry your way through it, or you learn to depend on God and bear it. In the midst of enduring, you learn to take your eyes off yourself and put them on Jesus. You learn patience and how to wait. You learn faith.

And faith breeds hope. When we experience God's presence, comfort, and faithfulness during hard times, we deepen our trust and hope in Him. We come to know with certainty that God is good. We *know* without a doubt He is in control and has a plan. We *know* God is faithful and loves us. And with this strong sense of faith, we can face any trial with hope—God is there, and He will see us through, all the way to eternity.

How well do you face suffering? What lessons has God taught you? What do you still need to learn?

Thank You, Jesus, for all my sufferings. I may not like them, but they do teach me a lot. Help me to face suffering well and grow in my faith. Amen.

"See, I have chosen Bezalel son of Uri. . .and I have filled him with the Spirit of God. . .and with all kinds of skills— to make artistic designs for work in gold, silver and bronze, to cut and set stones, to work in wood, and to engage in all kinds of crafts."
EXODUS 31:2–5 NIV

• • • • • • • • • • • • • • • •

You and your best bud—you like to do lots of things together, right? I mean, you'd get pretty bored if all you ever did was watch movies. There's no way you'd do the same ol' thing, at the same ol' time, *every* time you hung out. You'd both get tired of it.

God is a person, who desires to be in communication with you. And I'm pretty sure He gets bored when you spend time with Him doing the same ol' thing (reading your devotions and praying), at the same ol' time (in the morning or before bed), *every* time you hang out.

God creatively made you with special gifts and talents. What do you *love* to do? Play a musical instrument? Draw or paint? Write? Why not do that with God? Let your music, drawing, story, or art express your worship.

How can you have some fun hanging out with God today?

Wow, God, I never realized if I get bored spending time with You that You're probably bored, too! What new things do You want to do together? How can I get to know You in a new and fun way?

The LORD would speak to Moses face to face,
as one speaks to a friend.
EXODUS 33:11 NIV

. . . .

So we know we can talk to God, just like we talk to our friends. It doesn't have to be all formal and stiff, like we're addressing an honorable judge. We can just express ourselves to Him however we want.

But here's the kicker. . .*God talks back!*

Yep, you heard right. God talks back to you, just like a friend. Prayer is a two-way conversation. But how much chattering do *you* do? Can God get a word in edgewise? Do you even wait for Him to speak? Or do you just say your peace and then rush off?

It's pretty annoying when a friend talks your ear off. Lucky for us, God never tunes us out, but He also has some things to say. Do you take the time to listen? Some call this *listening prayer*—taking the time to be quiet, silent, and open to what God wants to say to us. God can communicate in an audible voice, but usually He speaks in a small, still way within our hearts.

When you're still and silent, what thoughts, images, or memories come to mind that speak deeply to you? Press into those and start your conversation with God.

Lord, what do You want to say to me today?

*You must worship no other gods, for the Lord,
whose very name is Jealous, is a God who is jealous
about his relationship with you.*
EXODUS 34:14 NLT

• • • • • • • • • • • • • • • • • • •

There was this girl I *really* wanted to be friends with.
She was just cool, you know? Great personality, fun to
be around, caring, and everything I wanted to be. And
we did become friends, but I was really insecure about
our relationship. I always felt like I cared more about
our friendship than she did. So I became jealous for her
attention. I wanted her praise, affirmation, and time more
than anyone else's—even God's. I put her on a pedestal
and looked to her for my needs, which she could never
fulfill.

Who do you put on a pedestal? Who are you
wrongly praising, elevating, and idolizing? In other words,
whose time and attention do you jealously want? It's
really easy to slip our eyes off Jesus and look to other
humans to meet the relational needs only God can fill.
Just as we grow jealous for other people's attention, God
grows jealous for ours. He wants to be—and is the only
one—Who can fully be everything you need.

*Lord, I look to You and You alone to complete me,
fulfill me, and love me. You are the perfect friend.
You're always there, all the time. I'm sorry for
depending on others for love and acceptance
instead of looking to You. Amen.*

Perfect Love

I love you, LORD; you are my strength. The LORD is my rock,
my fortress, and my savior; my God is my rock,
in whom I find protection. He is my shield,
the power that saves me, and my place of safety. . . .
He rescued me because he delights in me.
PSALM 18:1–2, 19 NLT

* * * * * * * * * * * * * * * * * * * *

Deep in our hearts, we long for love. We can't wait to marry someday and know the deep, abiding love of a husband. A love of someone who knows us intimately and that stands the test of time. A love that fiercely protects, humbly serves, and walks through fire for us.

This love that we long for. . .we already have. It's the love of Christ. He knows you more intimately than you know yourself. He created the universe and said it wouldn't be complete without you in it. He sees you at your best and at your worst—and loves you through it all. He gave up heaven for you—He *died* for you. He will never leave you and will always hold you, carry you, and protect you. . .because He delights in you.

You don't have to go searching for love—you already have it!

God, thank You for reminding me how much You love
me. No other love is perfect. No other love is as strong
or intimate. Any love I experience on earth is only a
reflection, a shadow, of Your great love for me. Amen.

Religion that God accepts as pure and without fault is this: caring for orphans and widows who need help, and keeping yourself free from the world's evil influence.
JAMES 1:27 NCV

• •

In 2004 seven Ugandan men met under a tree and prayed for God to send someone to bring hope and restoration to their war-torn country. God answered by calling Dr. Tim and Janice McCall to move to Uganda in 2005. They bought land around the tree where the men had been praying, and in 2007 Restoration Gateway was built.

Two and half million orphans fight to survive in Uganda, and Uganda has the highest rate in the world of kids being orphaned from parents who die of AIDS. One in seven children die by the age of five. Restoration Gateway runs an orphanage and employs widows to serve as house parents. Kids are clothed, fed, given a clean and safe place to play, and receive an education and medical care. They also employ men and women to work on the grounds, teaching them a trade and job skills, and they aid the local church with a number of ministries.

To learn more about Restoration Gateway (and how to sponsor a child or donate clothes and supplies!), visit www.restorationgateway.org.

God, thank You for hearing prayers and sending Tim and Janice to Uganda. Please continue to provide for Restoration Gateway so they can reach more and more Ugandans. Grow Your church in Uganda so more people can know You. Amen.

Imitate God, therefore, in everything you do,
because you are his dear children.
EPHESIANS 5:1 NLT

• • • • • • • • • • • • • • • • • •

Who's your model? Who do you look to for the latest fashion and hairstyles? Whose behavior do you find yourself imitating? Who do you follow on Twitter and wish you could be like?

We often mimic the people we want to be. They influence us because we value their opinions. Paul tells us in Ephesians to imitate God. I mean, *obviously* we need to model God because He's perfect. But that's not the reason Paul gives. We're told to imitate God because we're His children—His *dear* children.

We naturally want our parents to be proud of us. Their praise and approval meets our need to be loved and feel secure. When we obey them and model their example, we feel their pride in us. We are their precious daughter, and we make them happy!

As God's daughters, He delights in us when we imitate Him—following His example and obeying His commands because we want to please Him, because His opinion matters to us. Every earthly role model will fail us, causing disappointment and disillusionment. But God wants to be for us what others fail to be. So let's look to Him more than anyone else. Let's mimic God as our top model because we are His daughters!

God, I want to imitate You not just because I should, but
because I want to make You proud. Amen.

Show me your paths and teach me to follow;
guide me by your truth and instruct me.
You keep me safe, and I always trust you.
PSALM 25:4–5 CEV

· · · · · · · · · · · · · · · · · ·

You have heard the expression: *"When one door closes, another one opens."* Think about doors. They don't open on their own. Most of the doors that you encounter on a daily basis are not automatic. They require someone to open them! If you are a Christian, God is always at work opening doors for you. At times, when He knows what is on the other side is not best for you, He will close a door. As you pray for God's will in your life, you will become more aware of the opening and closing of doors. You may want to attend a certain school, become a member of a particular group, or be elected to a leadership role. Trust the Lord to open the right doors for you. You only see one piece of the puzzle at a time, but God sees your whole life as a completed jigsaw puzzle before Him. He already knows how the pieces will fit together. When you face the disappointment of a closed door in life, remember that God will open another one. The doors your heavenly Father opens before you are always the right ones.

God, sometimes I am so sad when an opportunity passes
me by or when someone else seems to get the things I
desire for my own life. Remind me that You are at work
behind the scenes. Help me to trust You more. Amen.

"If you become willing and obey me, you will eat good crops from the land. But if you refuse to obey and if you turn against me, you will be destroyed by your enemies' swords."
ISAIAH 1:19–20 NCV

. . . .

Choices bring consequences—big or small, known or unknown. For example, choosing to babysit often earns the reward of being paid. *Cha-ching!* Choosing to text your friends instead of studying for your math test often results in a lower grade. Good choices lead to rewards, and bad choices will (eventually) lead to destruction.

Our relationship with God is the same. If we are *willing* and *obedient* to Him, we prosper. But if we are *rebellious* and *disobedient*, life will get bumpy. This promise doesn't mean our obedience will *always* be rewarded in a comfy-cozy way. (Jesus obeyed the Father to die on the cross!) But God *does* promise that if your heart is willing and surrendered to Him, if you obey Him no matter what. . .He will bless you abundantly and lead you to better things. But if you insist on doing things your way. . .things aren't going to work out too well.

What choice will you make today?

Lord, help me to make good choices that honor You. Help me to be willing and obedient instead of selfish and stubborn. Amen.

Be merciful to those who doubt.
JUDE 1:22 NIV

. . . .

Do you ever have doubts about God? Questions you're afraid to ask? Maybe you feel like voicing your doubts makes you a bad Christian, that your faith isn't very sure if you doubt God. You should just believe, and these niggling doubts and questions are bad, so you stuff them down and hide them.

It's *okay* to have doubts, questions, and concerns about God. Know why? Because doubts make you take a closer look at God. And taking a closer look often leads to growth in your spiritual life and a stronger faith. Jesus doesn't want you to have a blind faith, where you just accept everything about Him because you're told that it's right. Jesus wants you to have a *trusting* faith, where you know Him and His character enough to trust Him without hesitation.

What niggling questions bother you about God? How do you have problems trusting Him because you doubt Him? Dive in to the Bible, ask your youth leaders at church, talk with your parents, and read Christian books until you find satisfying answers. Don't shove your questions aside—wrestle with them until you understand God in a new and deeper way!

God, help me find answers to my questions and resolve my doubts about You. Use my wondering thoughts to help me know You better. Amen.

*Keep the Sabbath holy. You have six days to do your
work, but the Sabbath is mine, and it must
remain a day of rest.*
EXODUS 31:14 CEV

• • • • • • • • • • • • • • • • • • • •

God created the Sabbath as a time to unplug. No
working, no cooking, no chores of any kind. Just a time
to gather collectively for worship and to rest and relax.

How well do you unplug each week? Traditionally,
we reserve Sundays as a Sabbath, but your Sabbath
can be on Saturday or any other day of the week (if you
don't have school!). Do you fill up your weekends with
sporting events, homework, friends, and activities? Even
if you're home and not running around, do you spend
your "resting" time glued to the TV, computer, or phone?
Instead of interacting with your family or spending time
with God, do you stay occupied with Facebook, texting,
and other types of social media?

Challenge yourself to unplug this week. Instead of
staring at a screen, spend time with your parents and
siblings. Have a game night. Read a book for fun. Take
a nap. Go for a walk. Take time to slow down and break
your normal routine and habits.

*Lord, it's so easy to stay busy. Even in my downtime,
it's easy to spend hours watching TV, messing around on
the computer, or scrolling through my phone. Help me
to unplug from my daily life and spend meaningful
time with my family and with You. Amen.*

"What must I do to inherit eternal life?" . . . [Jesus] said to him, ". . . Sell everything you have and give to the poor, and you will have treasure in heaven. Then come, follow me." When he heard this, he became very sad, because he was very wealthy.
LUKE 18:18, 22–23 NIV

· · · · · · · · · · · · · · · · ·

When we seek to follow God, when we pray and listen for His voice, do we really want to hear what He has to say? It's easy to pray when all we do is talk to God and ask Him for things. But it's a little more uncomfortable, maybe even scary, to quiet our hearts and be still, listening for God's voice and accepting what He has to say.

What are you afraid to hear from God? What stands in your way of fully following Him? How has your spiritual growth halted because you're afraid to hear what He might be asking of you? God isn't a harsh person who will always demand hard things of you, but following God does come with a price: You have to be willing to surrender everything.

Are there things you love more than God—things you're not willing to give up? Will you take the risk to hear from God and follow Him?

God, is there something in my life that's become more important than You? Is there something I need to surrender so that I can follow You? Amen.

April Frazier has published more than 50 articles in national magazines and book anthologies such as *Guideposts for Teens*, *Brio & Beyond*, and *God's Way for Teens*. Her readings can be found on pages: 9, 12, 13, 16, 18, 21, 25, 28, 32, 33, 37, 38, 42, 43, 44, 48, 54, 55, 61, 62, 68, 71, 74, 75, 76, 80, 81, 86, 87, 94, 96, 98, 99, 103, 104, 107, 108, 109, 110, 114, 115, 117, 118, 119, 120, 121, 122, 124, 125, 126, 127, 128, 129, 130, 131, 132, 133, 134, 135, 136, 138, 139, 140, 141, 143, 144, 145, 146, 147, 148, 149, 150, 151, 152, 153, 154, 155, 156, 157, 158, 159, 160, 161, 162, 163, 164, 165, 166, 167, 168, 169, 170, 171, 172, 173, 174, 175, 176, 177, 178, 179, 180, 181, 182, 183, 185, 186, 187, 188

Glenn A. Hascall is an accomplished writer with credits in more than one hundred books, including titles from Thomas Nelson, Bethany House, and Regal. His writing has appeared in numerous publications around the globe. He's also an award-winning broadcaster, lending his voice to animation and audio drama projects. His readings can be found on pages: 10, 11, 14, 15, 17, 19, 20, 22, 23, 24, 26, 27, 29, 30, 31, 34, 35, 36, 39, 40, 41, 45, 46, 47, 49, 50, 51, 52, 53, 56, 57, 58, 59, 60, 63, 64, 65, 66, 67, 69, 70, 72, 73, 77, 78, 79, 82, 83, 84, 85, 88, 89, 90, 91, 92, 93, 100, 101, 102, 105, 106, 111, 112, 113, 116, 123, 137, 142, 184

Scripture Index